NORFOLK
MAYHEM AND MURDER

NORFOLK

Mayhem and Murder

Classic Cases Revisited

Maurice Morson

Wharncliffe Books

First published in Great Britain in 2008 by
Wharncliffe Local History
an imprint of
Pen & Sword Books Ltd
47 Church Street
Barnsley
South Yorkshire
S70 2AS

Copyright © Maurice Morson 2008

ISBN 978-1-8415630-49-2

The right of Maurice Morson to be identified as Author of this Work has been asserted by him in accordance with the Copyright, Designs and Patents Act 1988.

A CIP catalogue record for this book is available from the British Library

Typeset in Plantin and Benguiat by
Chris Harris

Printed and bound in England by
CPI UK

Pen & Sword Books Ltd incorporates the Imprints of Pen & Sword Aviation, Pen & Sword Maritime, Pen & Sword Military, Wharncliffe Local History, Pen and Sword Select, Pen and Sword Military Classics and Leo Cooper.

For a complete list of Pen & Sword titles please contact
PEN & SWORD BOOKS LIMITED
47 Church Street, Barnsley, South Yorkshire, S70 2AS, England
E-mail: enquiries@pen-and-sword.co.uk
Website: www.pen-and-sword.co.uk

Contents

To the memory of
Willie Hobson,
policeman, fireman and gentleman

By the same author:

A City's Finest
The Lost Years
A Force Remembered
Rough Justice
Norwich Murders

Acknowledgements

My thanks go to the people of Norfolk and to all with an affinity with the county who helped in the research for this book. Whether you informed, provided, guided or read draft manuscripts, and the list below cannot possibly be all-embracing, I am grateful for the help afforded. In appreciation I mention the following:

Carole Howlett QPM, Chief Constable of the Norfolk Constabulary (now retired); John Mason, Peter Billingham and Peter Pilgram, Norfolk Constabulary archivists; Clive Wilkins Jones and staff of the Norfolk Heritage Centre, Norwich Millennium Library; Susan Maddock, principal archivist, and staff of the Norfolk Record Office; Tim Pestell, Ruth Burwood and Norma Watt of the Norwich Castle Study Centre; Dora Cowton, archivist of St John the Baptist Cathedral, Norwich; Ralph Lindley, Ripon Police Museum; Sid Drew of Denver; Colin Tooke and Les Cole of Great Yarmouth; Richard Le Cheminant, Dennis Durrant and the Gorleston GOSH Group; Michael Holness and Mavin Shulver of Thwaite St Mary; Amy Capon; Lorna Gillin; Peter Tadman; staff at the Great Yarmouth Library; the council divisions of the Norwich and Great Yarmouth cemeteries, and staff at the National Archives.

I pay special tribute to Ivor Warner, retired Great Yarmouth police officer and local historian, broadcaster and lecturer. His knowledge proved invaluable, his willingness exampled by walking me around Gorleston to explore the geography of the 1909 Alger murder. Sadly, Ivor died shortly afterwards.

In relation to the Alger murder I am grateful for the help given by David Alger and George Popay, relatives willing to share painful family memories.

My special thanks to Edna Sharpe of Denver for her courtesy and permission to explore a 170-year-old murder scene and for the information and picture she so readily supplied, and similarly to Ian and Nicola Carter of Thwaite St Mary, who readily allowed access to a scene of nineteenth-century murder.

There have been many students of the Burnham murders but Bernard Phillips, Cindy Stimpson and Peter Scholes were extremely knowledgeable and helpful. I thank them for their time and invaluable assistance.

Illustrations based upon research were provided by Terry George and David Rowlands, retired police officers and accomplished artists. I thank them for their skill in representing events in a pre-photographic age.

I am grateful, as always, for the skilled aerial photography of Mike Page.

The computer expertise of Neil Morson kept this book on course and I extend to him my thanks.

Illustrations throughout the book are source or copyright credited where they can be singularly and unreservedly defined. Some defunct newspapers can be attributed to the corporate responsibility of Archant (Norfolk) Ltd and I acknowledge the company's co-operation in respect of their past and present newspapers.

To all who helped, named or otherwise, thank you, this is your book as much as mine.

Maurice Morson

Introduction

Hindsight can be wonderful and cynical, emotionally revealing and educational, and a veritable searchlight on the past. These pages contain historic crime, and the reader is invited to be detective, judge and jury, criticising or empathising with those who went before, perhaps coming to new conclusions. I have researched and reinvestigated from a background of major crime investigation, applying the present to the past to clarify cases that scarred Norfolk long ago.

Norfolk Mayhem and Murder begins in 1829 with a workhouse murder and the first man to be hanged at the Norwich City Gaol, concluding in 1912 with the body of a pretty eighteen-year-old girl on a Great Yarmouth beach, her murderer unknown and now surely beyond the reach of justice. Three of the cases reviewed occurred before Norfolk had a professional police force; the remainder reflect the tortuous progress of policing in a class-ridden, hard-driven and strongly spiritual age. I have tried not just to record but to analyse with the benefit of knowledge denied to our forebears. Such thoughts and opinions that permeate this text are for the reader to accept or discard as he or she wishes. I found the research thought-provoking; may the reading be similarly described.

CHAPTER 1

Before the Police

Murder in the Workhouse, 1829

The man handed a paper parcel into the workhouse and hurried away, beginning a sequence that would both horrify and fascinate thousands. It was February 1829 and the city of Norwich comprised narrow streets and yards with an increasing number of people living hand-to-mouth in squalid conditions. The workhouse offered relief of a sort; it also meant stigma. Many destitute citizens sought outside relief rather than endure the disgrace and discipline of the feared building in St George's Bridge Street. Thomas Briggs had little choice. He was stricken with cancer, his face ravaged by the disease, feeding through a tube and needing constant care. And in his pain and loneliness in a crowded building he had another reason for despair. His wife lived away from the workhouse, visiting at intervals of anything between a week and three weeks, and she had recently announced she was pregnant by another man. Soon life for the ailing Thomas Briggs would get even worse. His was the name on the parcel.

Before a recognised police force, law and order in the city was the responsibility of ward constables (elected, often reluctant, citizens), the Night Watch (similarly untrained guardians), magistrates, the gentry, the church and, in emergencies, the militia. The great and the good investigated and adjudicated. Criminals usually came from the lower classes, victims of the station in life to which they were born and committed. John Stratford was different. He had an untarnished reputation, respected as a family and working man and described as 'more cultivated than is generally the case with persons in the labouring trade'. His strong physique gave a clue to his occupation as a smith.

Born in Postwick near Norwich of parents described as 'agricultural peasantry', Stratford received little if any schooling but learned to read and write in days when many could not, becoming an apprenticed blacksmith. He worked at Ludham and Seething and in 1817 moved to Norwich, where he became landlord of *The White Swan* public house in King Street, only to decide there was a better living in his original trade. In 1829, aged forty-two years, he lived with his wife and six children in a small house in St Faith's Lane, working from there as a whitesmith but also using a smithy in King Street. In a supreme irony he helped to build new gallows in the city.

Reasonably well-off in impover-
ished times, with strong family ties,
Stratford should have been content
with his lot. His downfall was another woman. He formed an intimate
relationship with Jane Briggs, wife of
Thomas Briggs, who was languish-
ing in the workhouse. Jane,
described as 'beholding to the eye',
had children of her own and had
known Stratford since 1822 through
the acquaintanceship of their respective families. The intimacy between
them formed after Thomas Briggs
entered the workhouse in May 1828.

Late in 1828 Jane Briggs found
she was carrying Stratford's child
and they contemplated two ruined
marriages and social disgrace. He
gave her money 'on account of her
situation' and hoped she 'would not

John Stratford

go her time'. He also gave her some pale brown powder to take. She did
not take the powder but agreed not to divulge the identity of the father
of her forthcoming child. In early February 1829 she was more than
halfway through her term and had to tell her husband of her condition.
She did not disclose the identity of the father. This perilously ill man
could do no more than accept the news with feelings of despair.

Jane Briggs always insisted that she never told Stratford she had
informed her husband of her condition. It made no difference; Stratford
determined to kill Thomas Briggs, a man he saw as a threat to his reputation and well-ordered family life. He may have salved some conscience
by seeing Briggs as a dying man to be hastened to his end.

How to murder, without detection, a man you could not approach without others being present posed a problem. And the means to effect death
had to be resolved. The answer to one gave the solution to the other: use an
innocent third party and an undetectable poison, which had to be arsenic.

Murderers of the time readily resorted to arsenic, known in high
society as the 'poison of kings', and elsewhere as 'the king of poisons',
also, for obvious reasons, 'the inheritance powder'. Women sometimes
used a form of arsenic as a cosmetic and there was even talk of it being
an aphrodisiac and a cure for the common cold, but it was more often
used in toxic form to destroy vermin, of which there was no shortage in
the poor living conditions of the time. The benefits for embryonic
murderers were its unrestricted sale, the absence of a proven method of

detection in the human body, and symptoms in death not dissimilar to other diseases, notably cholera.

Charles Cross kept a chemist shop in King Street and knew Stratford. In January 1829 Stratford came to his shop speaking of a problem with rats and wanting to know which of crude and powdered arsenic was the stronger. Cross advised that crude was more powerful than powdered but it was academic because he had only the powdered sort in stock. Stratford purchased powdered arsenic, the amount later to be in dispute, and the serving assistant, William Dawson, wrote 'poison' on the enclosing paper. Thomas Colman, a brazier, witnessed the transaction. He had been in Stratford's shop on business when Stratford said rats had got at a sack of his flour and he needed some arsenic and, as Mr Cross liked to have a witness to such purchases, he would appreciate the favour of him coming to the chemist with him.

On 11 February, Susan Hooke, a twenty-year-old kitchen servant at the workhouse, became aware of a man at the window of her kitchen. He was wearing a black apron and carrying a brown paper parcel, which he laid at the edge of the window, tersely announcing that it was for 'Mr Briggs'. She asked if she should ask permission for him to personally deliver the parcel and he replied she could 'take it just as well', making the issue *fait accompli* by walking away.

The parcel, bound in twine, 'Thomas Briggs' written on the front, lay undisturbed for an hour, eventually pointed out by Hooke to the workhouse nurse, Rhoda Burgess. Hooke explained the delivery and Burgess felt the parcel and guessed it contained flour. She took it to Briggs's room, where he lay in his bedridden state, with her husband, John, a shoemaker, sitting alongside. Briggs asked if the parcel contained money, and on being assured that its softness excluded any such munificence, he lost interest. John Burgess opened the parcel to reveal that it truly contained flour and Briggs grouchily commented that he already had an ample supply. Rhoda Burgess put the parcel in a cupboard.

Thomas Briggs regularly received flour from his wife, and occasionally from his daughter, delivered personally to him or left at the workhouse. Stratford had learned this when he had asked Jane Briggs how her husband was faring. His polite interest in Thomas Briggs's condition now changed to acute anticipation, and puzzlement as nothing happened. Thomas Briggs lived on.

Rhoda Burgess worked and lived in the workhouse with her husband and child, and on 2 March her husband drew attention to Briggs's parcel, saying that it was about time it was used. Shortly before dinner she saw him making dumplings and found that he had taken it upon himself to use flour from the parcel. She saw what she called 'a dirty white froth' on the water in the saucepan and initially declined to partake of a cooked dumpling but her husband ate heartily with apparent enjoyment, which persuaded her to eat two pieces. She gave portions to her young son and to inmates Mary Morse and Ann Pillar.

All five dumpling-eaters fell violently ill, John Burgess by far the worst. He told the hastily summoned doctor, John Coleman, that he was dying and pointed to what he believed to be the cause – the dough used for the dumplings. He gasped that his sight was failing and he had been poisoned, though whether he meant by design or accident he did not say. The workhouse surgeon, James Robinson, attended but Burgess died at six-fifteen that evening. The others slowly recovered.

The sudden death of a cancer-stricken man may not have excited the authorities' interest, as Stratford must have envisaged, but the rapid and agonised demise of a previously healthy man, accompanied by identical if lesser symptoms from four other persons after a meal, and with the dying man talking of poison and pointing out the offending substance, was another matter. Great excitement and concern followed the death of John Burgess. The workhouse's Court of Guardians ordered an investigation. Poisoning threw up fear of the unknown, posed questions of how and why, sent gossips and rumourmongers into a frenzy. But first, the nature of the poison had to be confirmed.

An eminent surgeon, William Dalrymple, conducted a post-mortem, originally saying he found 'arsenic in considerable quantity in the body', later backtracking to a position of safety in 'the possibility of arsenic'. He delivered the stomach contents to a chemist, William Stark, renowned for his experimental work on poisons. Stark also received the dough and the parcel, and a basin of flour from the cupboard in Briggs's room. An inquest upon the death of John Burgess was arranged for the following day, 3 March.

Things had gone wrong for John Stratford, and one may wonder whether Jane Briggs had any knowledge of or complicity in his evil plan. There is no evidence that she knew. She saw Stratford on the evening of Burgess's death, at her house at about eight o'clock, when he asked her to meet him later at his workshop. She refused. Before that she had not seen him for a week.

The next morning, the day of the inquest, Stark concluded that the dough contained arsenic, and he arrived at a similar but less firm opinion in respect of the parcel and stomach contents, the latter having been diluted by draughts of water given to the dying man. The flour from the basin in the cupboard was found to be uncontaminated, apparently part of a consignment from Jane Briggs.

John Stratford and Jane Briggs were arrested that morning, protesting their innocence. For Stratford it was the beginning of the end. Constable Isaac Kemp and John Bilham of the Court of Guardians searched his house and workshop and in the workshop found the wrapped arsenic sold by William Dawson. Handwriting found in the house matched the writing on the parcel delivered to the workhouse.

Jane Briggs gave evidence at the inquest, held at the Court of

Guardians, admitting her infidelity: she really had no choice. Further evidence came from Susan Hooke, Rhoda Burgess, Charles Cross, William Dawson, Thomas Colman, James Robinson, John Coleman, John Bilham and Constable Kemp, and experts William Dalrymple and William Stark. The inquest went into a second day, when the coroner and jury adjourned to the workhouse and the bedside of Thomas Briggs. He said that he did not know or suspect who had sent him the rogue parcel. Yes, he did know Stratford but he had not seen him for twelve months.

Stratford wished to address the inquest and began to dispute Susan Hooke's identification, saying his apron was different to the one she had described, but a solicitor came forward and advised him to say nothing at this stage. Stratford took that advice.

The coroner, Mr William Wilde, advised the jury that, when considering their verdict, they should bear in mind that it was of no consequence that the poison was intended for another person. Stratford may have seen the survival of his intended victim as some kind of mitigation, even salvation, but murder is defined as killing with malice aforethought. A plan to murder remains a plan to murder, even when it goes wrong and kills the wrong person. John Stratford was a failed murderer, but a murderer all the same.

The jury conferred for a quarter of an hour and returned their verdict: 'Wilful murder against John Stratford.' The coroner acted in lieu of magistrates and committed Stratford to the next Assizes for trial. He ordered Jane Briggs to be released. The city, buzzing with excitement, waited in great anticipation for a full exposition. The *Norwich Mercury* reported, 'We scarcely ever remember any case which caused more immense interest.'

The trial began at the Norwich Assizes on the morning of Friday, 14 August 1829, before Mr Justice Parke in a specially extended courtroom at the Guildhall. His lordship had earlier reviewed the case before a Grand Jury, saying, 'It is the greatest charge that can be made against a person, that of administering poison to another,' adding, 'It is not necessary for the poison to have taken effect against the person to whom it was intended.'

At nine o'clock Stratford appeared in the dock in a packed courtroom, the doors closed against many who, reluctant to leave, swelled the outside crowd. He pleaded 'Not Guilty' and was represented by three barristers, Mr Kelly, Mr Austin and Mr Palmer. Two barristers, Mr Alderson and Mr Preston, appeared for the prosecution.

The prosecution, apparently unsure of the jury's reaction to murder by mistake, had framed an indictment of each-way bets. In addition to the charge of murder they included counts of administering poison with intent and administering poison likely to cause harm.

The witnesses gave evidence much as they had at the inquest, but with more depth and slight variation according to the questioning of the defence and judge. Jane Briggs emerged unscathed in veracity, if tainted in reputation. William Dawson identified his handwriting of the word 'poison' and said that Stratford had asked for one ounce of arsenic but it was shop policy not to sell less than twopenny amounts. Charles Cross said, 'I think I sold him about two pennyworth of arsenic, which did not exceed two ounces.' More will be heard on this point.

The defence had no argument with most of the circumstances. What they had to dispute to save their client was his identification as the deliverer of the parcel and, if that failed, the relationship of the poison to the parcel delivered and placed in the cupboard. To this end they attacked Susan Hooke.

The kitchen girl may have seemed likely to waver in cross-examination, and perhaps sow seeds of doubt in the jury's mind by giving equivocal, hesitant answers. If her identification of Stratford became doubtful the prosecution would be left with sketchy circumstantial evidence allied to a hazy motive. In another century fingerprints would be taken from the parcel and the paper traced to source, straightforward forensic processes that would have amazed all concerned in this case. It didn't matter. The young woman identified Stratford in the dock – he had delivered the parcel; she was sure.

Mr Kelly accused Susan Hooke of changing her evidence. He claimed she had previously said the parcel man stayed two minutes and she was now saying he had stayed five minutes, and she had become mixed up on the time of the delivery, he said. She steadfastly denied changing her evidence or becoming confused. Counsel tried another tack. He took her on a geographical tour of the kitchen, homing in on the position of the window and the door, which opened to the yard. He asked how long the parcel had remained untouched at the window and where she had been during that time? And who had come into the kitchen? She said she had been present with the parcel the whole time it had been in the kitchen, thus defeating that line of questioning. Mr Kelly asked if she was subject to fits, knowing that she was. She agreed she was sometimes afflicted but said her fits did not last long and were being controlled by a doctor, James Robinson. 'No,' she told her inquisitor, she had not had a fit in the kitchen that morning. Counsel had no more questions. The young witness had conducted a stoic response to a severe cross-examination. Her evidence had not been dented.

Evidence of the presence of arsenic was not resisted by the defence, possibly because the opinion of experts is best countered by other experts and the defence did not have any. William Stark said that his experiments indicated arsenic in the dough and, to some extent, in the stomach contents and paper parcel.

William Dalrymple helped the defence a little by saying he thought the victim died from an 'acrid poison – *believed* arsenic', which he qualified even further by adding, 'This opinion I desire to express more cautiously.' The defence could have asked him to agree that there was no incontrovertible method of proving arsenic in the human body. They didn't.

John Coleman (doctor was not used as a title in those days) gave evidence of tending the dying man with warm water and Briggs saying, 'I'm poisoned. I am dying. It is no use.' Coleman thought that death arose from 'a mineral poison'.

The defence made some progress towards doubting the continuity of the parcel when Rhoda Burgess agreed that it had been left in an unlocked cupboard for three weeks, but the judge nullified this progress by asking her to describe the entrance from the street to the workhouse (there was a plan before the court) and she described outside gates and a gatekeeper with two inner gates. She said that she slept next to Briggs's room and persons visiting Briggs had to pass her room.

Two persons identified Stratford's writing on the parcel. One of those, James Wright, agreed that he was bankrupt and in dispute with Stratford.

The judge decided that Thomas Briggs should give evidence and ordered that he be brought from the workhouse, by stretcher or chair if necessary. He arrived, carried into court, speaking with difficulty, his face covered by a veil to hide the effect of his cancer. In swearing the oath his voice failed to carry and the judge agreed that surgeon James Robinson should act as interpreter. Briggs said he had been on good terms with Stratford, at which point Stratford, who had previously been composed, trembled and perspired, seemingly close to tears. Briggs's evidence tallied with that given to the inquest and the defence did not seek to antagonise the court by cross-examination.

The judge invited Stratford to speak and received the reply, 'I am perfectly innocent and I deny entering the premises of the workhouse in my life.'

Eight persons came forward to give evidence of Stratford's good character and the unlikelihood of him committing such a dastardly crime, most if not all of them esteemed in business or the church.

Mr Justice Parke began summing up at four o'clock but stopped when Stratford fainted. Stratford recovered and the judge continued.

The judge's summing-up lasted nearly two hours. He reviewed the evidence of each witness, identifying defence and prosecution points. The prosecution case remained as solid as it began. How solid the jury would decide.

The jury retired at five minutes past six, and at ten o'clock they sent a note to the judge. He called them back and said, 'The question you wish to put to me is whether or not it appears in evidence that any flour was taken from the bag before the dumpling was made by Burgess? The answer is there is no evidence.' (So the jury had considered the continuity and contamination or otherwise of the parcel.)

The jury, having received the judge's answer, indicated they were ready with a verdict. It was: 'Guilty!'

Stratford called out, 'I am innocent.'

The verdict was hastily conveyed to the crowd outside, some inside the building opening windows to be first with the news. Those inside waited in hushed expectation for the doom-laden words that must follow. The *Norwich Mercury* gave a striking account, reporting, 'The lurid glare of candles contrasted with thick and dark multitudes gazing with the stillness of death, giving a gloomy character to the scene.'

Mr Justice Parke told Stratford:

> The jury before whom you been tried have no doubt of your guilt, I entertain none, and there is no person who has attended to the details of the case who can entertain any doubt whatever .... God alone can be the judge of your motive ... you have no hope of mercy and have but a few hours to live.

He sentenced Stratford to be hanged on Monday at twelve noon and his body to be dissected.

There is a report that as Stratford left the dock he said to nobody in particular, 'I had a hand in it, but not in carrying the flour; although I know who did.' This utterance was ignored. It was over. He had two and a half days to live.

Stratford was returned to the city gaol at twelve midnight in an 'exhausted state' and, according to one report, the governor, Robert Paraman, stayed with him in his cell until three in the morning.

If Stratford expected his last weekend on earth to be peaceful, with time for contemplation and recuperation, he was to be sorely disappointed. The next day, Saturday, 15 August, he received a succession of visitors, mostly official and religious. The sheriff and under-sheriff came together and read from the Bible, and the Mayor, Mr T O Springfield, came to provide similar counselling; various men of the church came, some now anonymous though the name of the Reverend J B Innes has survived in record. Joseph John Gurney of Earlham Hall, a prominent crusading Quaker, member of the Barclay banking family and brother of Elizabeth Fry, the prison reformer, visited twice.

The official and religious zeal normally accorded to a condemned man had been stepped up. During Bible readings in his cell he was urged to speak the truth and told it was his duty to God, to society and himself. This would not be unusual, for great store was placed upon confession from those facing death, not so much as confirmation of convicting the right person but as repentance, redemption and salvation of the soul, and the public liked to hear of a repenting confessor. But the clue to the fever of activity around Stratford is contained in the fragmented reports of the interviews and, most notably, in a booklet written and issued by J J Gurney. This booklet is less an account of Stratford, his crime and demise, more a sermon advocating dedication to the church and its teachings, warning against the perils of sin as committed by Stratford. The booklet was initially free, instantly in demand, many copies grabbed as they left the printer's shop. An issue of 10,000 failed to satisfy a voracious public and a further 10,000 were printed and sold at a price of one penny a copy. A third or more of the city's population acquired copies, eager to learn more about an infamous murderer and his beliefs. It was these beliefs more than his crime that spurred the unusually numerous pre-death visits.

Books had been seen in Stratford's house and workshop during the search for evidence and their titles were reported to the authorities, the report moving on with the speed of outrage. The books were described as 'blasphemous'. The fact that the possessor of these books could no longer have recourse to them and would shortly take any blasphemous feelings he might have to another world was not sufficient. He had to repent and the books had to be removed lest they corrupt others.

How many 'blasphemous' books is not recorded but three authors were identified. 'Carlyle' can only be Thomas Carlyle (1795–1881) and 'Paine' must be Thomas Paine (1737–1809, born at Thetford, Norfolk), religious and political philosophers, radical then but viewed differently today. There is a confirming report of Paine when Stratford in interview attributed his troubles to reading *The Age of Reason*, a book for which Thomas Paine was imprisoned. The third author's name is noted as 'Hone' and this is surely William Hone (1780–1842), who was acquitted three times in 1817 of publishing matter parodying the church and government. It is interesting to note that in 1823 Carlyle wrote a dissertation in which he mentioned killing by arsenic.

J J Gurney, in his autobiography, saw Stratford's crime as

> an awful example of the effect of those dreadful publications, which are employed by the enemies of religion to sap the principles of the working classes.

He described interviewing Stratford 'in private' and finding him to be 'a man of strong understanding and warm feelings.

Stratford at first resisted efforts to cleanse his soul though he said he was satisfied with the justice of the sentence. This was seen as pleasing – the authorities always liked to release news of a satisfied condemned man.

A confession did come, reputedly as the sheriff read from the Bible with Stratford listening in quiet reflection and then pouring out his guilt and shame, admitting all that had been alleged against him. He renounced the 'infidel publications', as he allegedly called them, and asked that they be taken from his house lest his children see them and be corrupted – all dutifully reported by the press and J J Gurney.

Saturday was a day of repentance, drama and poignancy. In the afternoon Stratford's family were allowed a farewell visit and over a period of two hours he saw his wife, six children, two brothers and their wives and three distant relations. The parting from his wife and children affected observers and cannot be better described than through the *Norfolk Chronicle*, which reported that the youngest child, aged four years, 'overjoyed at seeing her daddy again, clasped him round the neck and with infantile simplicity of affection invited him to go home to tea.' Stratford wept after parting from his wife and children. He spoke of their uncertain future and his wife's 'delicate condition'.

Stratford's confession came verbally on the Saturday. He put it in writing on the Sunday. This account is best served by reproducing the confession as written.

16 August

I acknowledge the justice of my sentence, and that I deserve to die. It is not that I purchased two ounces of arsenic from Mr Cross; I purchased only one ounce, for which I paid two pence. I knew from my conversation with the woman Briggs that she was in the habit of sending flour to her husband in the workhouse, and she had said to me, what a blessing it would be if God would release him from his sufferings: from this and knowing that she was in the family way by me, and having in my possession about a third part of an ounce of crude arsenic, which I received from a person for whom I worked, I powdered it, sifted it through a piece of rag into some flour, which I put in the bag produced at the trial, tied it up, and directed it to Briggs. I then took it on Wednesday

The front of Norwich City Gaol 1827–1881, a unique picture. Stratford was hanged on this roof before a large crowd. Archives, St John the Baptist Cathedral

the 11th February last, about eleven o'clock in the forenoon, to the workhouse, and delivered it to the girl Hooke at the kitchen door of the workhouse, into her hand, in the expectation that it would be given to Briggs, and that he would partake of it. I did not go into the kitchen. I told her it was for Thomas Briggs; it did not occur to me at this time that I was committing any crime, but when I went to bed such terrors seized my mind that I could not sleep; I would have gone to the workhouse the following morning and got back the bag with its contents, but I thought it must have been used before that time, so I declare most solemnly that I did not make any use of the ounce of arsenic purchased off Cross, and that it was found in the same state as I first had it; my object was to destroy Briggs, from the fear that exposure of my intimacy with the woman Briggs would break the peace between my wife and me. I also declare that the evidence given against me on my trial was, with the variation appearing above, substantially correct. When I delivered the parcel to the girl Hooke she said she did not know Briggs; there was a lesser girl sat by the kitchen fire, who said Briggs was along with Nurse Burgess. Hooke asked me if I would like to carry it up by myself; I said no – I would rather not, and came away. Neither the woman Briggs nor any other person knew of my mixing the arsenic and flour, nor of my taking it to the workhouse.
Witness my hand
John Stratford

The above was read over to John Stratford, and signed by him in my presence
C F Millard
Chaplain at Norwich Gaol

This is a confession of striking inconsistency and confusion. The piece 'it did not occur to me at this time that I was committing any crime' does not sit easily with 'my object was to destroy Briggs'. And the statement 'I purchased only one ounce' is at odds with Cross and Dawson selling two pennyworth, 'which did not exceed two ounces'. The weight of the purchased arsenic bothered Stratford so much he decided that a postscript to his confession was necessary.

I, John Stratford, do firmly believe that if Charles Cross and William Dawson had not sworn falsely at my trial that I should have been set at liberty – but I freely forgive them as I hope God forgive me.
John Stratford

Witness, Edmund Newton, Under Sheriff
C F Millard

So Stratford alleged that Cross and Dawson gave wrong evidence leading to the right result – for justice if not for him. His claim that the purchased arsenic 'was found in the same state as I first had it' should properly have been made at his trial. The prosecution had been content with proving the sale, not the amount sold against the amount found, which brings up the most puzzling question of all. If Stratford already had some arsenic, why did he purchase some more, in whatever quantity, thereby creating a trail of evidence to the murder he planned? The answer went with the man.

News of a confession prompted a desire for another. Public opinion had cast Stratford as an arsonist as well as a murderer, seemingly because he had been first at the scene of a recent conflagration that had destroyed the *Steam Packet* public house in King Street. It was rumoured he had been in dispute with the landlord. He may have been first there because the *Steam Packet* was close to his own premises. The landlord, Thomas Watts, did not speak of any dispute but did suspect Stratford, possibly because of the rumours and the belief that a murderer would have no compunction in burning down a public house. Watts approached the authorities asking that Stratford be interviewed about the fire. They obliged and Stratford denied he was responsible, saying he was on good terms with Watts and the fire had probably occasioned from a furnace. He asked that, as a dying man, his name be cleared of any suspicion of arson.

On the Sunday Stratford asked to see the governor's children and this was allowed, according to the *Norfolk Chronicle*. These were indeed strange times! Whether the children knew of his fate is not known. The *Norwich Mercury* may have missed the meeting with the governor's children but made up for it by reporting that the governor's wife visited Stratford and spoke kindly to him. He spent a great part of that day reading the Bible and attending chapel, and he was allowed to speak to other prisoners, apparently urging them to take note of his folly, renounce their sins and follow the path of God. This information seems to have been released specifically for public consumption.

Stratford had his philosophical moments. He told one solicitous visitor, 'Here I am, a man capable of any effort and tomorrow before this time I shall be cut up,' and to the governor, perceptively, 'I suppose you have gone to London in search of someone to execute me.' The governor had indeed been to London to secure the services of William Calcraft, an executioner in the first year of a long and infamous career, to become loathed for his 'short drop' of only three feet, which often strangled rather than swiftly killed by breaking the spinal column, something that neither Calcraft nor the authorities were too concerned about.

When Stratford was offered blankets in his cell he supposedly replied, 'Ah, I shall be colder tomorrow,' pausing before adding, 'Well, no matter, it is a disease we catch but once.'

William Calcraft, executioner.

At five o'clock on the Monday morning people began assembling in the road opposite the new city gaol at St Giles, determined not to miss the first execution there (which was destined to be the only public execution there). Morbidity joined with a sense of history as they awaited the appearance and death of the most infamous murderer the city had known in a lifetime. Their number quickly grew, jostling and competing for the best viewing positions as the morning advanced. The narrow roads outside the prison walls were soon crowded to the disadvantage and eventual elimination of horse-drawn traffic.

At a quarter past nine workmen appeared on the flat leaded roof at the front of the gaol and began erecting the scaffold. At ten o'clock Stratford walked to the prison chapel and saw it standing starkly on the roof, commenting, 'Ah, there it is. I little thought when I saw it before that it was myself who was doomed to suffer upon that drop.'

After the chapel service the press reported that he said farewell to fellow prisoners, shaking hands through bars and telling them to repent their ways. It was said he gave his possessions to other prisoners, which may have foiled any claim from the executioner who was certainly entitled to his clothes. (William Calcraft would also augment his earnings by selling pieces of the rope he used, though it was said that sometimes what he sold exceeded the length he had used.)

At eleven o'clock the bell of St Peter Mancroft in the city centre began tolling its solemn message. The crowd had now reached several thousand, stretching back into St Giles Street as far as St Giles Church, people crowding into windows and upon roofs, walls and any suitable vantage point.

Some of the procedures that followed were described with journalistic enthusiasm and we can only marvel and recoil at the attitudes prevailing at the time, not just that of the ghoulishly waiting and swelling crowd but of officials steeped in pomp, prolonging the anguish of a doomed man – though the doomed man was in no hurry.

A few minutes before twelve noon Stratford approached the lodge from the prison infirmary with a retinue of officials and press, his arms pinioned by William Calcraft, 'walking firmly with a steady countenance' according to one report, and 'looking worn and woe-begone' according to another. The press reported that at the Porters' Lodge he shook hands with the governor, chaplain and others, and indeed there was to be much handshaking after pinioning, which invites further explanation. Calcraft used a waist belt to pinion the elbows to the torso and tied the hands at the wrist in front of the body. The quality of the handshakes can be imagined.

An observant reporter noted that as Stratford walked across the prison yard he spotted a female face pressed against a window and called out, 'Goodbye, God bless you.' The governor's wife, perhaps?

The procession climbed from inside the lodge to the roof to be greeted by cheers from a sea of upturned faces. A short ladder led to the gallows. Stratford knelt in prayer or contemplation at the foot of the ladder. The rooftop assembly waited quietly, the crowd noisily.

Stratford rose to his feet and was asked if he had anything to say, a procedure that would later be discontinued.

He replied, 'No, sir, nothing whatever; my work is nearly done.'

He climbed the ladder and from his heady position turned and faced the multitude staring up at him. He bowed to them three times and turned to the waiting hangman, coming to attention as Calcraft strapped his legs and placed the white cap and rope over his neck. In a moment of chilling farce he told Calcraft the rope was the wrong way round. Calcraft responded, 'No, never mind. Stand right.' In this moment of blindness, on the point of death, there were, reportedly, more hand-shakes. He shook hands with Calcraft, and then the governor again, to whom he said, 'God bless you, sir, and all your family – I thank you for all your kindness.' Then the head turnkey stepped forward to shake hands and say goodbye. The keenly watching and listening press report-ed that Stratford began reciting the Lord's Prayer and 'beseeching forgiveness'.

A handkerchief was held up for the crowd to see: the handkerchief dropped, the trapdoor opened and John Stratford plunged downwards; after a few tremors he was still. The bell at St Peter Mancroft stopped its mournful toll.

John Stratford was dead but his sentence remained incomplete. After hanging in view of all who cared to look for the customary one hour he was taken down, stripped and placed in a shell, then taken to the Guildhall and placed on view in the Lower Court. He remained there for two hours, thousands filing past to view the punishment of a murderer.

After the public viewing the body was taken to the Norfolk and Norwich Hospital and given to the supervision of Mr Dalrymple, to become the focus of lectures, examinations and demonstrations. The *Norfolk Chronicle* thought it proper to report the medical findings but the details they so assiduously carried will not be material to the reader of this account. John Stratford became the last in Norfolk to suffer the final indignity. The sentence of dissection no longer applied after 1832.

The tragedy and consequences of murder reach beyond the murderer and victim and there was public compassion for the plight of Stratford's wife and six children, one of whom had touched hearts by inviting her father home to tea. Unusually, a public subscription sought to help the murderer's family; history does not say how much it succeeded, or whether Rhoda Burgess received any help.

Norwich Guildhall, where Stratford was tried and his dead body exhibited for public viewing. Norfolk County Council & Information Services

CHAPTER 2

Before the Police

Riot, Acid and Arson, 1830

It was the worst of times and the very worst of times. A city and county lurched from open discontent to revolt in the streets, fields and farms, a rising tide of enmity accentuated by the class divide. Weavers and agricultural labourers, burdened by the realisation of the present and a fear of the future, rose against employers and authority. England had experienced living and labour problems after the Napoleonic Wars, but in Norfolk, from late 1829 to early 1831, simmering unrest and protest gave way to riot, assault, arson and attempted murder as looms overtook the handwork of weavers and threshing machines replaced men toiling in the fields. Unemployment or less than a living wage threatened. Mechanical progress made men desperate, fostering anger, leading to hatred, leading to violence.

A warning of the extremism to come occurred on 22 December 1829 when a group of men, estimated at twelve strong, their faces covered in black cloth and coloured handkerchiefs, burst into the home and workshop in St Augustine's, Norwich, of cloth manufacturer William Springall. They threatened to shoot anybody who resisted them. Springall, anxious for his wife and children, did resist and was shot in the stomach. He fell, bleeding profusely. The raiders stormed into the workshop and cut off the cloth from seven looms, leaving as quickly as they had arrived, ignoring the man lying in a spreading pool of blood.

A surgeon, who was quickly on the scene, stemmed Springall's blood loss and saved his life although his condition remained 'precarious' for some time. The last report available says the surgeon was unable to extract the slug. Springall did, however, recover. The *Norfolk Chronicle* called the shooting 'an outrage so unenglishman like'.

Alarm over the shooting of Springall translated into special meetings of magistrates and a plea to Robert Peel, Home Secretary and founder of the Metropolitan Police, for help. He replied with a letter of advice and apologies for not attending in person due to other commitments. He authorised a reward of £100 for the capture of the gunman and a King's Pardon for the accomplices.

In January 1830, a letter to the *Norwich Mercury* bemoaned the 'distressed and unsettled state of the city', a state heightened by the newspaper reporting that weavers had declared they were prepared 'to die in the streets'

A reward and pardon authorised by Robert Peel.

£100 REWARD

And his MAJESTY'S FREE PARDON.

Whitehall, Dec. 28th, 1829.

WHEREAS it hath been humbly represented unto the King, that, about half-past Ten o'clock on the night of Tuesday, the 22d instant, a large number of Persons attacked the House of WILLIAM SPRINGALL, in the Boatswain's Call Yard, in the Parish of Saint Augustine, in the city of Norwich, and with great violence broke open the said House, and several Men entered therein, one of whom FIRED a PISTOL at the said William Springall, and seriously wounded him in different parts of his Body, and afterwards some of them Cut the Work off Seven Looms in the said House, and committed other Acts of Violence.

His Majesty, for the better apprehending and bringing to justice the persons concerned in the offences before mentioned, is hereby pleased to promise his most gracious pardon to any one of them (except the Person who Fired the Pistol) who shall discover his accomplice or accomplices therein, so that he, she, or they may be apprehended and convicted thereof.

Signed ROBERT PEEL.

And as a further encouragement, a Reward of

ONE HUNDRED POUNDS

Is hereby offered to any person (except as aforesaid) who shall discover his accomplice or accomplices therein, so that he, she, or they may be apprehended and convicted thereof.—The said Reward to be paid by the Treasurer of Norwich.

and that 'constables have been directed to perambulate the city.' At the City Sessions the chairman opened by regretting the absence of the 'tranquillity that usually prevailed'.

The countryside joined the city in a groundswell of protest. Agricultural labourers had their own cause to promote. Threshing machines were leading to acute poverty among those who were already poor. Before the year was out the agricultural labourers would be in open revolt, but for the time being they rumbled their discontent through protest meetings and occasional machine-breaking and stack-burning. A severe storm and coastal flooding on 10 January curtailed some of these rural protests.

On 12 January 1830, Henry Willett, a cloth manufacturer, was recognised in Tombland in Norwich and surrounded by a 'hooting and hustling mob'. A passing magistrate, Colonel Harvey, went to his aid and was hit by a stone. Undeterred, he thrust into the crowd and grabbed the stone-thrower, retreating with his captive and Willett into the Cathedral Close, slamming the gate against the crowd. More magistrates arrived, greeted with stones and brickbats. Two more men were arrested. Magistrates read the Riot Act and worked their way through the seething crowd to deliver their prisoners to the city gaol at St Giles. Willett escaped unhurt. Stone-thrower John Burrows, who had injured Colonel Harvey, got three months' imprisonment.

Later this same day there came a concerted attack upon the workhouse, where new looms had been delivered for use by the paupers. A mob, estimated at 3000 strong, invaded the building in St George's Bridge Street and the looms were pitched into the river – conveniently adjacent to the building. The mayor and magistrates sitting in petty session in the Guildhall were interrupted when Robert Martin, a ward constable, burst in and reported the 'city in a state of insurrection'. The mayor suspended proceedings and hurried to the workhouse

A lesser reward notice describes an attack upon an aptly named family.

accompanied by several magistrates, but order was only restored, and then slowly, when a troop of Dragoons arrived from the Cavalry Barracks. The following day would see another alarming incident, murderous and personal.

Cloth manufacturer John Wright lived in St Faith's Lane, a dark, poorly lit (gas lamps arrived later that year) street with pockets of complete blackness. Nearing his home between nine and ten o'clock in the evening he was confronted by a shadow that detached itself from the overall gloom. He had a split-second view of a human shape holding a bottle before his vision disappeared into a fury of heat and blinding pain. Sulphuric acid swept over his face. Staggering in shock and agony he pursued his attacker, drawing a pistol and firing wildly before collapsing and crawling to a nearby house.

The fact that Wright was carrying a pistol may be indicative of troubled times and his fear of violence. The press described his injuries as 'dreadful'. In one report he lost the sight of his right eye, in another he lost the sight in both eyes. The *Norwich Mercury* said, 'The blood runs cold at the contemplation of such atrocity.'

City magistrates distributed notices offering a £100 reward to whoever identified Wright's assailant, and the mayor sent for an 'experienced officer from Bow Street', almost certainly acting upon Robert Peel's advice. The Metropolitan Police had commenced patrols in London on 29 September 1829, following the crime-fighting team known as the Bow Street Runners, set up in 1749 by Sir Henry Fielding. The Bow Street Runners did not restrict their activities to London, ranging into the provinces to detect treasonable and other major crime. Their records show that they came to Norfolk seven times. Mr Ellis, Metropolitan policeman, and probably a Bow Street Runner before that, duly arrived from London. There is also an account of Chelsea Pensioners arriving to assist the city authorities keep the peace. (Chelsea Pensioners of this time were fit and active retired military men.)

Mr Ellis made enquiries but what he found, suspected or did has become submerged in vagueness and lack of record. His work may have been laudable, and indeed several persons were arrested (and released) for the attack upon Wright, but we cannot measure his progress with any certainty. He may have suspected Richard Nockolds of perpetrating the attacks upon Springall and Wright.

Richard Nockolds, a 34-year-old weaver, married with five children and another expected, was becoming a leading light among recalcitrant weavers. He was not disposed to public speech-making but given to regular rebellious meetings in private houses with the like-minded, and was free speaking to his own sort, heedless of those who might be disloyal. He should have been known to the authorities.

A twentieth-century Special Branch would certainly have known about Nockolds. Intelligence-gathering through informants and witnesses, and snippets of careless talk from the growing public disorder would have collated suspects and ringleaders by description or name. But the policing of Nockolds' day was an extraneous duty for citizens such as magistrates and ward constables. Nockolds would eventually answer for the attacks upon William Springall, John Wright and others, though not to a judge and jury. Justice would visit him through another route.

Unrest and trouble in the city and county subsided during February as deep snow limited activities, legal and otherwise. Severe weather can be as effective as any police force. The problems, however, remained.

August 1830 saw a General Election that led to more fractious assemblies. John Morse, a 38-year-old bricklayer with a wife and two children (it was reported his wife had lost nine other children), attended a meeting in the Market Place and was struck by a stone during rough-house electioneering. He died six days later and an inquest recorded a verdict of

murder. Unsurprisingly, the offender was never discovered.

The autumn saw a successive poor harvest after a wet summer, and the approach of winter meant more trouble on the land. This would be a time when agricultural labourers would rise up in concerted and organised violent protest, and not just in Norfolk. The 'Swing' riots swept over southern England (named after a legendary 'Captain Swing' who sent threatening letters to the authorities) and Norwich

Lying in wait with acid. Terry George

weavers would join them to perpetuate the fight against employers. At the same time England looked nervously at another revolution in France and uprisings elsewhere in Europe, only too conscious of its own troubles.

November 1830 is documented as the beginning the Swing agricultural uprising though incidents of fire-raising and damage had taken place over several previous years, exampled in Norwich as early as 1822 by three ex-soldiers, no longer needed by their country, firing a stack in protest at their deprivation. They were hanged at Norwich Castle.

On 10 November 1830 there occurred several incidents of machine-breaking and stack-firing throughout the county. On 13 November the owner of a burning stack at Briston appealed for help from a large group described as from the 'labouring classes' looking on. He was met with 'a sullen silence'. Imploring the watching men to help fight the fire, he received the reply: 'What is the use of our assisting? Whether it is burned or not will make no difference to us – we are as badly off as we can be, and it is impossible for us to be worse, therefore it may take its course.'

The situation deteriorated. By the end of the month stacks had been fired and threshing machines broken as far apart as Holt, Reepham, Hempnall, North Walsham, Caister, Beeston, Hindolveston and Thorpe. At one o'clock in the morning 150 men went to the farm of John Girling at Paston and called him up, saying it was their intention to destroy his threshing machine and they intended no personal violence, but if 'legal measures' were taken against them 'worse would follow'. They wrecked the machines and left, the farmer helpless to intervene.

At Hindolveston magistrates were quickly on the scene and, after reading the Riot Act, they rode their horses into the demonstrating crowd causing what the press described as a 'severe scuffle'. That scuffle led to seven men being detained and taken to the Walsingham Bridewell. Further machine-breaking took place at Walcott, Happisburgh, Scottow, Dilham and Burnham Thorpe. Stacks were fired at Mousehold and Thorpe.

In December a sawmill at Catton was burned down and machinery broken; threshing machines were destroyed at Hellesdon, Cawston, Haveringland, Dalling, Kerdeston, Hackford, Norton, Guestwick, Foulsham and Reepham. In Norwich the weavers weighed in by damaging factories and related premises at St Martin's and New Mills. How much intermingling of weavers, agricultural labourers and outside agitators took place is open to question; for certain all were involved in the big picture.

The cry of the rioters at one incident was 'more work, a larger loaf', and the attentive press, zigzagging through the county, reported 'they did not suffer to take a turnip' from the premises they attacked. At one countryside fire, farm labourers helped to douse the flames.

Magistrates read the Riot Act at different places, mostly to little effect. Fires and damage sometimes occurred, with indistinguishable figures melting into the darkness; sometimes a crowd stayed to encourage the fire; sometimes flames raged in an eerie silence following the visit of a band of fast-moving raiders, forty to fifty planting incendiaries and disappearing as quickly as they came. Some of those held by the hypnotism of the dancing flames or the compulsion to demonstrate were at risk from arriving magistrates, constables, the Yeomanry or the Dragoons. In many cases authority did not arrive.

There is a record that 1800 special constables were sworn in at Norwich and 'a course of defence arranged', whatever that was. Meanwhile, rampant and disaffected men revisited North Walsham, and hay-cutting and drilling machines were smashed. Threshing machines were damaged at Hickling and there was a report at Reepham of stones thrown by demonstrators. At Little Walsingham two men and a woman from Kent were arrested and identified as agitators promoting the national cause. At Leziate a man making demands of landowners was arrested. Fires broke out at Harpley, Ringstead and Raynham and at Lyng a paper mill burned down. Machine-breaking and disorder ringed Norwich at Taverham, St Faith's, Horsford, Hainford, Saxlingham, Barford, Bawburgh, Bowthorpe and Easton. A company of Dragoons assembled at Costessey as a response unit and from there a 'troop of horse' set out and arrested seven men, lodging them in the Wymondham Bridewell. Riots were recorded at Southrepps, Docking, Haddiscoe, Attleborough and Honing, and prisoners were taken at each of these places.

On 23 December, Sir Thomas Hare of Stow Bardulph put a night watch on his land. His men challenged trespassers who levelled three guns and roughly commanded, 'Back off'. Hare's men didn't back off and two guns fired, and a third jammed; James Weston fell dead. Seven men were arrested and charged with murder but none were convicted of that offence. Firearms and poaching offences were proved instead and the men were variously sentenced, the severest being seven years' transportation.

It seemed that the labourers were winning when magistrates in North Walsham issued a notice begging 'the owners and

Riot and arson occurred throughout the county.
Terry George

occupiers of land to discontinue the use of threshing machines and to increase the wages of labour to ten shillings for able-bodied men'. Some landowners publicly denounced the use of threshing machines but it was probably the number of arrests that lessened the incidence of disorder and destruction, plus the reduction of targets in stacks and threshing machines. The trouble had peaked rather than stopped. History records the national Swing Riots as taking place from 1830 until 1832.

Overall it was but a hiccup in the pain of mechanised progress, the long-term outcome inevitable, but Richard Nockolds no longer cared. Motivated by rebellious instinct and bitterness, he had been leaving his city to walk miles into the countryside to burn and wreck in a cause that was not his. But persistent criminals are vulnerable because of their persistence; Nockolds' time was nearing.

Norfolk County Sessions in January 1831 carried a heavy calendar of alleged machine-breakers and rioters. The press reported 'never so tremendous a list of prisoners'. Of 205 defendants 108 were charged with machine-breaking in November and December and 50 with riot. In addition, 9 cases of machine-breaking and arson had been sent to the Assizes.

The first case to appear before Chairman Sergeant Frere set the pattern for a bad-tempered administration of justice. Henry Dawson pleaded 'Not Guilty' to machine-breaking at Taverham, and after hearing the evidence the jury found him 'Not Guilty' because, they said, 'there was only one witness.' This upset Chairman Frere and he retorted that one witness was as good as one hundred and it was their duty to believe that one witness. This upset defence counsel Mr Palmer but Frere refused to listen to his protest. Mr Palmer called on the court to record the verdict. Chairman Frere called on the jury to reconsider their verdict. They said they would, retired and

A proclamation indicative of troubled times. Norfolk Heritage Centre

Guildhall, Norwich,

DECEMBER 4th, 1830.

The Mayor and Magistrates consider it to be a paramount duty which they owe to their Sovereign and their Country at this moment of general disturbance, to declare that, whilst in common with the rest of their Fellow Citizens, they are on the one hand ready to do all which sympathy and benevolence can suggest for the relief of distressed operatives in this populous place, so on the other hand it is their full determination to act with the promptitude, decision, and vigour, which circumstances imperatively demand, in prohibiting tumultuous assemblies, and suppressing riotous proceedings, in opposing every kind of open outrage, and actively endeavouring to detect secret attacks, on either Person or Property.

The Mayor and Magistrates are anxious to impress on the minds of their Fellow Citizens, that persons who are guilty of these lawless proceedings, are liable on conviction to suffer Death, and that the loss incurred by Individuals by the destruction of their Property must be paid by the Public, and will consequently tend to the increase of the County Rate.—Taking the present occasion therefore to acknowledge and applaud the zeal of numerous respectable Individuals, who in voluntary compliance with the summons already issued, have meritoriously come forward as Special Constables, the Mayor and Magistrates renew their call on every well-disposed Person, capable of rendering assistance, to enrol himself on the same list, being firmly resolved upon an organized and efficient employment of the Civil power, supported, if there should be need, with such other aid as is authorized by Law, for the speedy restoration of public tranquillity.

W. SIMPSON,
TOWN CLERK.

returned another 'Not Guilty' verdict. Applause rang through the court, further upsetting the chairman, who spoke of punishing the applauders. Dawson was discharged with ill grace.

Trials of alleged machine-breakers and rioters followed, presided over by an increasingly tetchy chairman. Of the 108 alleged machine-breakers 67 were found guilty. Of 50 charged with riot 23 were found guilty and 18 were discharged on entering into recognisances to keep the peace; the remaining 9 were acquitted, including all those charged with riot at Honing. The chairman responded to this verdict by commenting bitterly, 'The jury, for reasons best known to them, thought proper to acquit the prisoners.'

Sentences varied from a few weeks' imprisonment to transportation for fourteen years. Some were ordered to serve a week or two weeks' solitary confinement. A voluble chairman, speaking crossly about widespread lawlessness in the county, accused the press of supporting 'newfangled doctrines and theories'. This drew the editorial response from the *Norwich Mercury*: 'We can only attribute the undiscriminating vituperation of the press into which he has betrayed, to the long, to the exciting, and the painful task he has been subjected to.' The newspaper summed up by saying, 'The next twelve months are the very crisis of the fate of England.' The local future would be more civil unrest and damage, and stacks lighting up the countryside. On 25 January there came another acid attack.

Charles Green, a carrier, travelled to Norwich from his home at Tasburgh to buy yarn and at around nine-thirty in the evening he walked his pony and cart through the Harford Bridge tollgate carrying his purchase in a bag. Men suddenly rushed forward, throwing stones. They knocked him to the ground and beat him with hurdle stakes. One man pulled his head back and poured acid in his ear. The attackers stole his yarn, drove his cart away, which was later found in pieces, and released his pony.

Two weaver brothers, Hardy and John Shepherd, were arrested for this new acid attack. They had spoken of Green's collusion with manufacturers, openly enquiring of his movements, and supposedly expressing a desire to murder him. Yarn sold by Hardy Shepherd was identified as that stolen from Green. The brothers were charged with highway robbery.

Green appeared in the witness box at the Assizes with his face covered, his appearance 'weak and disabled' and his hearing 'nearly lost'. He could not, or would not, identify his assailants and expert witnesses disputed the identification of the exhibited yarn. The brothers protested their innocence and five witnesses gave them an alibi. The judge summed up by saying that if the jury were unsure that the yarn produced in evidence was the yarn stolen from Green they must acquit. The jury deliberated for half an hour and found the brothers guilty, but recommended mercy. The judge demanded to know the grounds for their recommendation. The jury foreman replied that they didn't believe the recovered yarn was the stolen yarn, whereupon the judge refused to accept their verdict. He ordered them to retire again and they did so, for two hours, again returning a verdict of 'Guilty', but without any recommendations. The irritated judge sentenced the brothers to death. By a quirk of fate their destiny now lay with Richard Nockolds, himself now in custody.

Nockolds had been charged with two counts of arson involving straw, wheat and barley stacks belonging to farmers William Blake and Richard Ducker at Swanton Abbott. The evidence on these counts had much in common but they were to be heard separately, although the first verdict would presuppose the second.

A weakness in getting away with crime is the fallibility of accomplices, and Nockolds had plenty in his many offences. In this case of alleged arson his companions were charged as accessories. They were Josiah Davison, aged twenty-one years, David Davison, aged twenty-six years and Robert Hunt, aged thirty-one years. A third Davison brother, Robert, stood apart, intent upon saving his life as the principal witness for the Crown. If the prosecution had had a better case he would have been in the dock with the others.

How Robert Davison cut his deal is not known. There is nothing to say he was paid a reward, which doesn't mean he wasn't, and how he came to notice in the first place is also unknown. Intelligence emanating from previous incidents could have made him and others, particularly the rousing Nockolds, suspects. A tip-off may have led to him. It is possible that he was the tip-off, the author of the downfall of the Shepherd brothers, but, whatever the truth, a participating villain now stood for the Crown.

On the morning of Friday, 25 March 1831, the four defendants stood before Mr Justice Alderson at the Norfolk Lent Assizes. The first count against them named farmer Blake. The prosecution sought to call their prime witness, Robert Davison, but the judge wanted to know more about a witness with more qualifications for the dock than for the witness box. The committing

Another acid attack.
Terry George

magistrate, the Reverend W Blake, was called before the judge to explain Robert Davison's transformation. He assured Mr Justice Alderson that no kind of deal had been done or promise made and that Robert Davison had voluntarily offered to be a witness without inducement (the underlying inducement was his life). After a lengthy cross-examination of the magistrate the judge allowed Robert Davison to be called.

Robert Davison said that Nockolds called at his house in St Augustine's in Norwich twice on the same day and had meetings with his brothers, Josiah and David, and Robert Hunt. He said Nockolds asked about stacks that had not been fired and produced a ball of cotton with a tail, which Nockolds claimed would burn for half an hour to get a stack going. He then gave a demonstration in the hearth of the ball's burning power. Farms around Swanton Abbott fell under discussion.

As the villains plotted, there came an insight into their respective roles, as told by Robert Davison. He said that Josiah proposed a payment of five shillings to Nockolds, with a further payment of half-a-crown if his brother David would contribute. This suggests that Nockolds was for hire, a man contracted for his incendiary ability; but apparently Nockolds said he was not doing it for money.

They agreed the targets, stacks belonging to farmers Blake, Ducker and Wilson, and possibly farmer Massingham. Nockolds said he would do the actual firing. Robert Davison said he refused to go with them but later changed his mind. They agreed to meet in Norwich at six-thirty the next evening.

The next evening, a Saturday, was not the best for fire-raising – it was raining. Unfazed by the weather, the gang of five left Norwich at seven o'clock, Robert Davison armed with a pistol, which he said Nockolds gave him. Was this the pistol that struck down William Springall?

It was a scene that invited suspicion: a roughly dressed group of men shambling through intermittent rain along a pitch-black country road. As they were nearing Ducker's farm a man ran after them. That man, Aaron Cooke, was prompted by the group running and walking quickly away from him; but then two of the men turned back and one asked him the way to North Walsham, a mistake by Nockolds.

Cooke gave the necessary directions and Nockolds, having got directions he didn't need, faded into the darkness to rejoin the others; but he had created a witness. Cooke later saw a glow in the night sky.

Nockolds began placing incendiary balls in stacks. He had fifteen or sixteen such incendiaries, some obviously carried by the other men. He placed four or five in stacks belonging to Ducker, hurriedly leaving as men suddenly appeared. He went on to plant incendiaries in stacks belonging to Wilson and Blake, with Massingham spared for a lack of incendiaries. Robert Davison said that Nockolds 'dropped paper' near the farms of Wilson and Massingham and he queried the paper and was shown a handwritten note, of which more later.

The gang's return journey to Norwich halted about two miles from the stacks as Nockolds scanned the horizon and expressed disappointment that it remained as dark as ever. He wanted to go back and check the incendiaries but the others were against it, or so Robert Davison said. After another half-mile and the head-turning Nockolds noted with satisfaction a glow in the distance. What he didn't know was that Wilson's stacks had not ignited, Blake's had been only partially consumed and just one of Ducker's was burning. They got back to Norwich at four in the morning.

Robert Davison suffered in the witness box the contemptuous cross-examination afforded to turncoat villains but he stuck doggedly to his account and the truth remains the truth whatever the source. Whether it was the truth in substance, or a gilded variety, the judge left to the jury. Some corroboration came from Aaron Cooke when he identified Nockolds in court.

The jury's decision on all the defendants was 'Not Guilty'.

The Nockolds family were euphoric. They made arrangements for a 'frolic', as the press called it, to welcome home the head of the family, confident of a repeat verdict on the second count. But the prosecution had an ace to play.

The trial on the second count, firing stacks belonging to Richard Ducker, began with a new jury, and a surprise. The prosecuting barrister, Mr Evans, offered no evidence against David Davison and Robert Hunt and they were acquitted, seemingly recognition that the case was heading for early failure. Not so! The prosecution were after Nockolds and they attributed the notes left at Wilson's and Massingham's farms to him. A search of his house had found a writing book and Robert Martin, ward constable, had matched indentations in the pages to the writing in the notes. Comparing indentations, paper, ink, torn edges and handwriting, even fingerprints, would today be tasks for forensic experts. Martin's initiative stands out for its time – crushing evidence assumingly not used in the first trial because the notes were not found near Blake's farm.

Three identical notes had been found. One of them was produced in court along with Nockolds' writing book, both examined intently by the judge and jury. There seemed to be agreement that the impressions matched the writing.

The produced note, read in court, said: 'A reward of a hundred pounds will be of no use, for I have done it alone, and I can keep my own counsel. I will surprise you more than this before you are a year older. Keep that in mind.'

On the back of the note was written 'The Truth'.

The judge invited the defendants to speak in their defence. Nockolds responded by saying that Aaron Cooke had been mistaken, and the evidence of the indentations was worth nothing because his children had been tearing pages from the book and his lad had been working with Robert Davison. He pointed out that the jury had no evidence of his ability to write or his handwriting. He then addressed the jury thus:

> With respect to the accomplice to the Crown [Robert Davison] you, gentlemen, are well aware that he is not to be depended upon as an impartial witness. You know, gentlemen, that I was tried yesterday and the jury returned a verdict in my favour, and I consider your footsteps will fall precisely in the impression of their footsteps.

He finished by asserting his innocence and the inadequacy of the evidence against him.

Josiah Davison told the jury that his brother had 'sworn falsely' against him. He asked for mercy, which seemed an anticipation of the verdict.

The judge summed up and the jury retired, returning within minutes with a verdict against Nockolds of 'Guilty'. A cry from the public gallery caused Nockolds to request his wife be removed from the court before sentencing.

The jury next deliberated on the accessory charge against Josiah Davison and after fifteen minutes returned a verdict of 'Guilty' with a recommendation for mercy.

Mr Justice Alderson told the convicted men they had no hope of mercy (which must have lowered Davison's spirits after the jury's recommenda tion) adding, 'I beg of you, short as the time may be, diligently to apply yourselves to acts of devotion and prayer.' He advised 'contrition and penitence' and pronounced sentence of death before wearily sinking his head onto a cushion. In contrast, the *Norwich Mercury* reported that Nockolds 'exhibited a most disgusting levity of demeanour'.

Josiah Davison duly repented his crime, and some others, and, according to the press, became converted to the Christian faith. Richard Nockolds supposedly embraced the faith and admitted what the press called 'many atrocious crimes'.

Nockolds admitted a principal role in the attacks upon Springall, Wright and Green, adding that the Shepherd brothers were innocent. He admitted burglaries by intimidation and several cases of arson. As burglary was also punishable by death he had lengthened the odds on a reprieve, which could only come by Royal Prerogative or from the judge – and he had already declared his position.

The executions were scheduled for Saturday, 9 April 1831. Davison wrote a letter to his family and asked that it be read over his grave. There was no need. He was reprieved. Whether he would have been reprieved without repentance and conversion to the faith is open to speculation. The Shepherd brothers were also reprieved, sentenced to transportation and dispatched to Portsmouth on 6 June. The following month they were pardoned and returned to the city as free men.

Nockolds said his farewells to a tearful family knowing his life was spent. On the appointed Saturday, just before twelve noon, he stepped into the courtyard of Norwich Castle with the usual accompaniment of officials, of whom he calmly asked, 'Which way?' Passing observing magistrates, he bowed and said, 'I wish you good morning, gentlemen.' He was pinioned and led through the castle gates, briefly trembling as he saw the waiting crowd. He quickly recovered his composure and stepped firmly up to the gallows and, following the precedent set by John Stratford, whose execution he probably witnessed, bowed twice to the crowd. Nockolds was dispatched without preamble, watched by an unusually silent crowd.

Nockolds became the only man to suffer execution in Norfolk's Swing Riots. Some would suggest his role, whilst major, was no more culpable than others, notably Robert Davison, whose wife was later prosecuted for making incendiaries. Robert Davison can be considered fortunate to have escaped Nockolds' fate.

The *Norwich Mercury* expressed the view that the silence that greeted Nockolds' hanging was one of 'no excuse or extenuation, no pity, no regret'. The newspaper launched an attack upon the authorities for inquiries that 'lacked tact and energy', proffering the view that Nockolds should have been detained long before he actually was, claiming he was 'foremost in many acts of violence'.

The *Norfolk Chronicle* described Nockolds as 'a friend of sedition' and also thought he should have been caught earlier, significantly reporting 'so many did he confide his secrets', adding that he had 'a bitter hatred against every order of society above him'.

Was Nockolds really reviled by the local population, as the press thought he should be? The heavy silence at his execution, normally a rumbustious and noisy affair with hawkers, drunks and morbid revellers seeking entertainment in death, may have reflected a view of him as a crusader for the oppressed working classes, the execution seen as a victory for the ruling class. His vicious attacks with acid would have been overlooked, only the motives remembered.

The body of Richard Nockolds was given to his wife and she, enterprising woman, displayed it at their Barrack Street home, charging one penny for a viewing. She apparently made a considerable sum. He was one of the last to be so returned after execution. From 1832 the executed were buried in the grounds of the prison where they met their end, sometimes the body being displayed to other prisoners. After 1836 arson ceased to be a capital offence.

Nockolds' funeral was attended by his many friends, some undoubtedly accomplices, and the crowd was such as to reinforce the suggestion that he was more popular with the people than the press would like to believe. The mourners were led by his wife and children, the eldest a fourteen-year-old boy. They buried Richard Nockolds, rebel and cruel villain, at St James Church a few yards from his home. The church is now a theatre, perhaps a symbolic resting place for a man who held the stage of a city and county.

CHAPTER 3

Before the Police

The Burnham Poisoners, 1835

Death did not come easily to the innocent or the guilty in the case that history variously records as 'The Burnham Murders' and 'The Burnham Murderers', the plural correct in each title. The innocent suffered horribly, slowly, without knowledge and proper medical attention, declining in piteous despair under the real and supposed care of relatives and neighbours. They died unnaturally, victims of the poison of kings and the king of poisons.

The very word 'poison' shocks. Throughout time murder by knife, gun and blunt instrument has never attracted the same degree of revulsion as killing by poison, which is viewed as deceptive, sly and insidious, a disguised assault. The evil in this sordid tale typifies.

In the early nineteenth century vagrancy, poverty and austere living conditions manifested in the daily grind to live, eat and stay warm and healthy. Disease and a limited life expectancy ran through the century. The tale that follows has to be seen against this primitive and difficult backcloth, when members of a rural community in north Norfolk under-handedly, yet recklessly, sought to remove from this world those who should have been nearest and dearest to them. In some cases they were successful and such was the awfulness of their actions they became the focus of national attention. *The Times* of London observed, 'This county of Norfolk has seldom been in a greater degree of alarm and excitement.'

The Burnhams are a collection of villages within a few miles of Wells-next-the-Sea, variously named and variously known, Burnham Thorpe notable as the birthplace of Horatio Nelson, Burnham Market as the place where women committed murder. Today, tourists and wealthy second-homers frequent this idyllic part of Norfolk but in Burnham Market in 1835 (then more usually known as Burnham Westgate) three cottages joined and formed an entity with a carpenter's shop in North Street, next to a Methodist chapel, the occupying families maintaining the homespun, sociable and popping-next-door relationships usual to the time.

Frances (also known as Fanny) Billing, aged forty-six years, lived in an end cottage with her husband and eight children, the youngest aged nine years. She had originally borne fourteen children and the loss of six can only be ascribed to the infant mortality of those times. Frances came from Blakeney, the daughter of a shepherd, and had married James

Billing, an agricultural labourer, in 1808. She augmented the household finances by 'going out washing' and was described as a 'woman of no ordinary endowments', which may have referred to her build or her intelligence – the reader will find little evidence of the latter. She was, however, said to have 'strength of purpose' and the reader will find evidence of that.

Initially respected in Burnham Market as a regular churchgoer, Frances came to be reviled as a 'loose' woman. This looseness was specific and fuelled by keen observations and gossip. She had formed an intimate relationship with her next-door neighbour, Peter Taylor, and they were seen together after dark by villagers and twice confronted together by James Billing. He caught them in a back room at his home and on another occasion emerging from the privy that served all the cottages, following which he gave Taylor a hiding and his wife a black eye. This flirtatious and feisty woman responded by 'swearing the peace' against her husband and he was bound over to the Petty Sessions for abusing his wife.

The Taylors lived in the middle cottage. Peter Taylor came from Whissonsett and had married Mary Miles on Christmas Day 1815. They had no children and he was seen as a sober, steady man until 1833, after which he was so steady he did very little work; a 'layabout' was one description. By occupation he was a journeyman shoemaker, though he did not journey much or make many shoes and was, reputedly, dogged by ill health. There was to be a lot of ill health in the three cottages.

Peter Taylor occasionally earned money by waiting at tables and singing at the Independent Meeting House and the *Hoste Arms*. He and his wife were not too badly off in the context of the times, a state that owed much to the industry of Mary Taylor. She was between forty and fifty years of age, of good character, liked and respected. She worked as a shoe binder and may be seen as a woman to be admired in the company of those to be despised.

Catherine (also known as Kate) Frarey lived with her husband, Robert, and three children aged seven years, four years and eighteen months, as lodgers above the carpentry shop in the third cottage. Thomas Lake and his wife, Mary, ran the carpentry shop. Catherine was forty years of age, the daughter of 'poor but honest' parents in Wells, where she had been 'creditably brought up'. One description of her says she had 'no personal attractions whatever'. She had married Robert, seven years her junior, in 1823. He worked as an agricultural labourer in the parish of Burnham Overy except when he was ill, which is for the term of our story. He had previously been a fisherman.

Catherine had a respectable reputation at first in Burnham Market, but by 1835 she, like Frances Billing, was dubbed 'a loose woman'. Her association with a Mr Gridley became the subject of gossip and later more serious reference, but the most notable feature of Catherine's character was her devotion to 'drugs, charms and conjurations'. She believed in fortune-telling and the supernatural, and was a follower and associate of women who were regarded as witches.

Bizarrely, Catherine, despite her reputation for immorality and weirdness, worked as a childminder, taking young children into her home to nurse and school on account of mothers who wanted to work. Here lies the beginning of a line of tragedies.

During the afternoon of Saturday, 21 February 1835, Elizabeth Southgate, a 28-year-old farm worker, received news at her place of work that her six-month-old daughter Harriet, left in care at Frarey's cottage, was seriously ill. She hastened to the cottage and found the baby shrieking with pain. Robert Frarey accentuated the harrowing scene by lying moaning on his bed.

Robert Frarey had been unwell for two weeks and been treated by Hugh Rump, a doctor sent by Frarey's employers. Inflammation of the stomach had been diagnosed and a course of pills prescribed. That diagnosis would prove to be correct and the pills suitable, though not in the form he took them.

Elizabeth Southgate tended her child with a cup of warm water sweetened with what she took to be sugar from the Frarey household. Harriet fell silent, slept for quarter of an hour and awoke consumed by convulsions. This awful condition lasted until the early hours of the next morning when she died in her mother's arms. A distraught mother left to break the news to her husband. She had borne five children (one illegitimate) and only two remained alive.

As the child lay dead in her cottage Catherine Frarey continued to feed her husband gruel seasoned with a white powder 'sweetener'. His condition worsened.

Robert Frarey did not get better and the following day, Monday, Catherine Frarey and Frances Billing walked the five miles to Wells to consult Hannah Shorten, a fortune-teller and spiritual counsellor, or more accurately a charlatan and, in the eyes of many, a witch. It was said that Shorten believed in the power of white arsenic thrown on a fire to bring two lovers together. She had, two years earlier, counselled Mary Wright of Wighton with these beliefs, following which Mary's husband had died from arsenic poisoning. Mary had been convicted of murder, escaping the gallows on account of her pregnancy but dying in Norwich Castle before she could be transported. A popular view was that Shorten should have joined her.

Robert Frarey had been ill at the same time as Mary Wright's husband, when both wives were being counselled by Hannah Shorten, and he only got better because the other man died. Two deaths would have been too much, a cautionary view that appears at odds with the recklessness to come.

Catherine Frarey asked Shorten to 'look in a cup' for them. She obliged and advised of troubled times in Billing's and Frarey's families. Shorten asked, or was invited, to go to Burnham Market the next day, the purpose of the visit never fully explained. Accounts of the Wells meeting between the three women came from the women themselves. It is what has been left out the reader must speculate upon.

The journey back to Burnham Market by Catherine Frarey and Frances Billing created trouble. Peter Taylor met the women on the road outside the village and went off with Frances. Catherine arrived home alone, seen by James Billing. Half an hour later Frances arrived and, challenged by an angry husband, refused to explain her delay. Later she spoke in a rage and said she had walked in the dusk with Peter Taylor, nothing more. Her husband was unable to prolong the row because the next day he was laid low with stomach pains and feared he had contracted cholera. He got better after four days.

Harriet Southgate had died from natural causes according to the visiting doctor, though how the visible agony of the child could be so described is difficult to accept through modern eyes. But this was a time of high infant mortality and cursory inquiry.

Robert Frarey continued to fight his painful illness, aided by a robust constitution hewn as an all-weather fisherman. Catherine continued to feed him gruel.

On Tuesday, 24 February, Robert Frarey sat miserably by the fire and Elizabeth Southgate arrived for the start of the funeral of her child, enquiring of his health.

He replied, 'I am not so well.' Did he look at the tiny coffin on the nearby table as he spoke?

Hannah Shorten arrived, dividing her time between Billing's and Frarey's cottages. She had a whispered conversation with Catherine in Robert's presence but he was beyond taking an interest. Then Catherine picked up the coffin and outside the cottages there formed a sad and short line of those barely known to a desperately short life.

After the funeral service Hannah Shorten accompanied Catherine Frarey to check on the condition of her husband, Robert. As Shorten entered the cottage she announced, 'Dear me, here is a smell like a dead corpse.' Accepting that there is no other kind of corpse, her psychic powers were further dented by the discovery of Robert Frarey alive, peacefully sleeping. Getting better?

After the improvement in Robert Frarey's condition, if improvement it truly was, Catherine Frarey, Hannah Shorten and Frances Billing conferred in Billing's cottage, the result being the purchase of arsenic from the nearby pharmacy. There is a record that Billing asked Shorten to go with Catherine because Catherine knew the way and the name of 'the stuff', and Shorten would admit that she was so asked and did accompany Catherine. But the evidence of Samuel Salmon, the pharmacy apprentice, is that Catherine and Frances came to the pharmacy on 25 February, Catherine making a twopenny purchase of arsenic without explanation and Frances buying one pennyworth for rats and mice in her cottage. Salmon handed over white packets marked 'poison'. This cannot have been their first purchase. It would not be their last.

Hannah Shorten must have been involved in the discussions and decisions that followed, as limited as they may have been, because Catherine and Frances knew exactly what they were doing and killing rats and mice did not figure too highly. Shorten spent three nights at Billing's cottage, sleeping in the eldest son's room while he was away at sea.

On 26 February Elizabeth Southgate called at Frarey's cottage for her child's clothes, at the same time enquiring of Robert Frarey's health, which was not good. While she was there Frances Billing appeared with a jug of warm porter, swirling the liquid round before pouring it into a cup that revealed a white, settling sediment.

Southgate pointedly said, 'I should not take sugar in porter.'

Frances, unperturbed by the comment, gave the porter to Robert Frarey, urging him to 'drink it up'. He said he did not like the taste and she responded by saying it would do him good. He drank it and became sick and doubled with pain. The following day his condition worsened and Mr Rump arrived to again diagnose inflammation of the stomach.

Robert Frarey died on Friday, 27 February, racked with pain, crying that his sight was failing, his mother, sister, wife, Frances Billing and Elizabeth Southgate at his bedside. Never was there a more happy release.

In this tale of serious illnesses it is recorded that at the time of Robert Frarey's death his sister-in-law Sara at Burnham Overy was ill with similar symptoms. One account says that Catherine fancied her brother-in-law. Without police and medical methodology to investigate suspicious circumstances, or even see they were suspicious, these separate but similar events passed off unconnected. We shall never know whether Sara had indigestion.

The death of Robert Frarey did not provoke official interest or ring any alarm bells to those nearest to the sequence of illness and tragedy. Like the death of the child, it was accepted as the result of natural causes.

Peter Taylor went into Frarey's cottage to shave and prepare the corpse (his talents included barbering) and was greeted by Catherine, both unaware that Elizabeth Southgate was outside the door.

Catherine said, according to Southgate, 'Let's just bury him out of the way and there'll be some more of them dropped.' Taylor's reply, if any, was not noted.

After the laying-out of the corpse, Elizabeth Southgate again listened unseen as Frances Billing spoke to Peter Taylor.

'The doctor's been,' said Frances, 'and it's all right with him.'

Burnham Market (Westgate) in 2006. Top left: the murder cottages have gone, replaced by lock-up garages, but the chapel building next door, now a tourist shop, remains. Upper right: the pharmacy is still a pharmacy. Centre: The Hoste Arms, scene of inquest and inquiry. Bottom right: St Mary's churchyard, where the victims lie. Mike Page

'Good,' Taylor replied, 'then we'll go about her as soon as you like.'

They buried Robert Frarey in St Mary's churchyard and his wife wept over his grave.

On 7 March, Frances Billing asked an elderly friend, Jane Dixon, to witness a purchase at the pharmacy. Frances bought two pennyworth of arsenic saying it was for Mrs Webster at Creake. Mrs Webster would say that she knew nothing of the purchase. Frances gave Dixon one penny for her trouble.

The next day James Billing refused his Sunday dinner. His wariness did not extend to afternoon tea and after taking that he was sick. He remained ill for three days.

About this time James discovered that his wife talked to their bed-room wall and he found a flint could be removed to give speaking access to the Taylors' cottage. He hid under the bed to listen. Frances unsuspectingly removed the flint and whispered through the hole, 'I told you one more Sunday would finish our concern.' She arranged to meet Peter Taylor that evening after dark. There would be witnesses within the village to say they did meet.

Mary Taylor knew of her husband's infidelity, the whole village did, but she remained stoically loyal and unconvinced. This attitude may have changed if she had known of another of her husband's meetings with Frances Billing, again observed and overheard by the seemingly ever-present Elizabeth Southgate. Southgate saw Peter Taylor and Frances Billing coming from the cottages' privy, him handing her a white paper packet. Southgate heard Taylor say, 'That's enough for her.' This devastating revelation never appeared in evidence against Frances Billing – an omission to be discussed later.

On Thursday, 12 March, Mary Taylor went to work in apparent good health. She left dumplings and pork gravy to be warmed for dinner. On returning home she ate the warmed-up meal and became violently ill. Whether her husband dined with her, and of the same meal, is not apparent from the evidence. He would say that he did and was ill. For certain he did not suffer to the same degree as his wife.

Mary Taylor suffered through the evening as carers and other visitors, later to be witnesses or defendants, came and went. Frances Billing called, though whether it was to see Peter or Mary Taylor is not known; she had a motive for wanting to see both.

Catherine Frarey became a self-appointed nurse and her ministrations were intensive and transparent. By seven o'clock she was boiling gruel in her cottage for the sick woman, seen by Edward Sparks, brother of Elizabeth Southgate, who was looking for his sister on account she hadn't prepared his supper. He saw Catherine put white powder from a white packet into the gruel. She threw the empty packet on the fire. During that same evening Sparks saw Frances Billing wave out of the window and then go outside. He saw her meet Peter Taylor outside the privy, Taylor clapping his hand on her shoulder as he said, 'Never mind, she will soon be done away with and it will be alright with us.' In the prevailing situation it is difficult to put an innocent complexion on that statement, though it never appeared in evidence against Billing, and initially not against Taylor.

Phoebe Taylor, Peter's sister-in-law, called and Mary Taylor asked her to go next door and collect the gruel that Catherine was 'kindly' preparing. Phoebe went and was told by Catherine that the gruel needed seasoning and there was salt and sugar in the Taylors' pantry, and lump sugar should be used. Phoebe did as instructed but Mary could not take the gruel, saying it was too thick. Catherine then appeared and took the gruel away, returning a few minutes later, saying, 'It's thinner now and I hope you'll take it.' Mary took it.

Downstairs in the Taylor cottage William Powell, a blacksmith, sat waiting for a haircut from Peter Taylor. He offered to leave as he saw, in his words, 'women flitting in and out with bowls, cups and jugs.' Peter Taylor said he should stay and gave him a shave and haircut while Phoebe Taylor held a candle.

Powell saw Catherine come downstairs and place a basin of gruel on the table and put in 'powdered sugar or flour' on the point of a knife. She then put a large portion of what looked like salt in the gruel and carried the basin back upstairs.

Mary Lake from the carpenter's shop arrived to help care for the tormented, convulsing woman, and Mrs Miles, Mary's mother, also arrived. In the late evening Peter Taylor sat downstairs and asked the busy Catherine, 'How is she?'

'Very bad,' Catherine replied, 'but we have hopes.' A latter-day investigator would ask what she was hoping for.

To his dubious credit Peter Taylor asked Catherine to go for a doctor but she replied that it was 'no use' as she was 'too far gone'. He pleaded with her to go and she went, followed by Phoebe Taylor. They returned with Albert Cremer. He found Mary unconscious and said there was nothing he could do, but then struck the first note of alarm. He asked if there was any poison in the home, going downstairs to ask Peter Taylor if he was troubled with vermin.

Peter Taylor said they usually trapped rats and mice.

Cremer returned upstairs to find Mary Taylor had died.

Mrs Miles, Phoebe Taylor, Mary Lake and Catherine Frarey washed and prepared the body, after which they went downstairs to the waiting Peter, who had brewed a pot of tea. In a story littered with significant remarks there appeared another. Catherine pointed to the bowl of lump sugar and ungrammatically said, 'We didn't ought to have none of that.' They used powdered sugar supplied by Mrs Miles.

Catherine tipped Mary Taylor's unfinished meal of pork gravy and dumplings in the privy. Was she tidying up, or disposing of evidence?

Mary Taylor's death was the springboard for widespread suspicion and, more importantly, official inquiry. Three deaths within thirteen days in adjoining properties, all showing the same painful symptoms, had to be a matter of concern, even in times of privation and disease. The mention of poison locked into the existing infidelity scandal, and Coroner Francis Quarles ordered Francis Church, a Burnham surgeon, to conduct a post-mortem.

Once again the omnipresent Elizabeth Southgate takes pole position. She went to the Taylors' cottage to pay her respects, it is said, and joined in conversation with Peter Taylor and Catherine Frarey. This was no eavesdropping scenario.

Catherine said, 'I thought we should have got on, but now I don't know.'

Peter replied, 'I hope we shall' and, turning to Elizabeth Southgate, 'Have you heard anything about the coroner coming?'

'No,' lied Southgate. 'Why do you ask?'

'Why? Because they talk about opening my wife.'

'Opening your wife?' Southgate effected incredulity. 'Why would they do such a thing?'

She did not get an answer. She knew the answer. So did Peter Taylor and Catherine Frarey.

Post-mortems of the nineteenth century often took place in the building where the body lay and Mary Taylor, examined in her home, would be the silent yet best witness. Francis Church sliced open a swollen abdomen and pointed out to Albert Cremer the hideously inflamed stomach and bowel. He removed the stomach, tied it off, and took it to the pharmacy for examination by druggist Henry Nash, who knew enough to test for arsenic within the limits of the time. In his opinion the stomach was riddled with the poison.

Church, mindful of the continuity of evidence and difficulty of identifying arsenic in a body, personally took the stomach to Norwich, where surgeon Richard Griffin conducted experiments and tests with sulphate of copper and other agents before opining that the stomach was 'highly impregnated with arsenic'. (The ultimate breakthrough in absolutely proving arsenic in the human body came in 1836, using zinc and sulphuric acid, first proved in a criminal trial in Paris in 1840.)

It is reasonable to expect that at this time Frances Billing would keep her head down, so to speak. Instead, another death threatened and the circumstances were just as suspicious – more so in the light of previous happenings.

On the Sunday morning, with Mary Taylor lying cold and gutted next door, James Billing came home from church to find that his wife had cooked him a dumpling. He promptly lost his appetite, which upset Frances. He repeated village gossip that Mary Taylor had been poisoned, whereupon his wife flew into a rage, saying, 'They wouldn't harm her Pete' and 'She'd made sure of that' (without defining 'they' and 'she'), next threatening to 'do the business for him [her husband] before twelve months come to an end'. She vowed to swear the peace against him the next morning.

James rashly took some tea that day and noticed, too late, a white powder in the cup. He became very ill, Frances being unmoved by his pain. The following morning she went to the magistrates to once again swear the peace and found them busy. They were empanelling a jury for the coroner. They refused her request.

Catherine at this time was on her way to Wells to see Mr Rump, taking with her the attentive and persistent Elizabeth Southgate.

Elizabeth had said to Catherine, 'If I was you, Mrs Frarey, I would have my husband taken up and examined, to shut the world's mouth.'

Catherine had replied, 'No, I shouldn't like it.'

Catherine asked Rump if her husband had been poisoned but he merely confirmed his diagnosis of inflammation of the stomach. The two women moved on to Hannah Shorten, where Catherine said she would have to get back to Burnham for the inquest. Hannah Shorten, suitably primed, must have prepared herself for the inquiry to come.

Mary Taylor was buried in the churchyard next to Robert Frarey. There is little record of the mourners and their demeanour, suffice to say that all those close to Mary had much on their minds.

On the day of the inquest a woman named Elizabeth Ward called at the cottages to speak to Peter Taylor, and while she was with him Catherine Frarey and Mary Lake arrived. Ward heard Catherine say to Peter, 'There you are, Taylor, we should have both been done if it had not been for our mother [Lake's sobriquet]. God bless her; the gruel was boiled in mother's house.' Readers may make of this statement what they will.

The inquest took place in a crowded *Hoste Arms* on 17 March, described by the press as a 'long and patient investigation'. The jury concluded that Mary Taylor had died from poison 'administered by persons unknown'. The coroner referred the case to the magistrates and Frederick Hare and Henry Blyth held 'special meetings in consequence of certain rumours'.

Frances Billing was arrested on Wednesday, 18 March as she made her way to South Creake to see Mrs Webster, probably to bring her on side in relation to the arsenic purchase. She was questioned at the *Hoste Arms* and placed in a carriage to be taken to the Walsingham Bridewell, at which point Catherine unwisely called out, 'Hold your own mor' and they can't hurt us.' The significance of 'us' is overwhelming.

They arrested Peter Taylor the next day. As he was led through the public room of the *Hoste Arms* the persistently careless Catherine called out, 'There you go, Pete. Good luck! Hold your own and they can't hurt you.' At least she made this statement in the singular.

Catherine Frarey tried other means to subvert the investigation, demonstrating her fear and weird beliefs. She exhorted two of Frances Billing's sons to hire a pony and gig and drive her to see 'the wise woman of Salle' (another charlatan and reputed witch) in order that she might ask her 'to tie the prison keeper's tongue' to prevent him questioning their mother. The young men, Joseph and Samuel, asked if their mother was innocent and Catherine swore that she was. 'In that case,' they replied, 'why shouldn't she be questioned?'

Catherine was soon taken into custody, as was Hannah Shorten at Wells. The exhumation of Robert Frarey followed, the post-mortem conducted by Francis Church.

Robert Frarey, three weeks into his grave, had a well-preserved (a feature of arsenic), badly ulcerated stomach, which was duly removed and taken to Henry Nash and Richard Griffin, as before. Both men found, in their opinion, traces of arsenic.

Harriet Southgate was exhumed and some reports say arsenic was found, others say it wasn't. No charges would be brought in respect of this child, which may have produced the view that arsenic was not discovered. Opinion would have wavered on so small a body. It was probably present in a minute quantity – it would not take much to kill a baby. Her death would have resulted from contact with arsenic in the cottage but without any predisposed malice – a case of culpable homicide amounting to manslaughter. The evidence was stronger in respect of the adult deaths.

A search of Taylor's cottage gave up traces of arsenic in flour and sugar. An account says arsenic was discovered in the swill bin in Billing's cottage but Francis Church said he found only uncontaminated flour and paste there, which was something of a surprise to Frances Billing who, as we shall see, expected arsenic to be found in her bin. A dumpling, apparently the one refused by James Billing, was retrieved from the communal privy and found to be impregnated with arsenic.

Frances Billing, Catherine Frarey and Peter Taylor were committed to the Lent Assizes for trial. Hannah Shorten did not go to trial, which must have enhanced her reputation no end. She had not woven a spell of immunity, merely fallen short of the evidence required. A reviewer of the time described her as the 'presiding genius' in all that took place.

Frances Billing made what was loosely regarded as, even entitled, a confession. In fact it was a rambling document in which she placed all the blame on Catherine Frarey. She claimed that Mr Gridley wanted Robert Frarey 'put out of the way' and Catherine went with Shorten to buy arsenic to achieve that aim. Frances said Catherine also wanted arsenic to 'draw Mr Gridley to her at night'. She said Catherine put arsenic in the 'flour poke' at the Taylors' cottage and had given her contaminated flour to put in her (Frances's) swill bin. And, Frances claimed, it was Catherine who had given Robert Frarey arsenic in porter. According to Frances, Catherine said 'there shall be more of them dropped', naming Mary Lake.

Catherine denied any wrongdoing, as did Peter Taylor.

The Assizes in April at Norwich saw Frances Billing and Peter Taylor appear before Mr Justice Vaughan. Defence barristers informed the judge that Catherine Frarey lay ill in the Walsingham Bridewell 'in such a state she was unable to be moved'. Rumour had it she had been poisoned. Other accounts speak of a mental and physical breakdown.

The judge reluctantly agreed to a postponement to the Autumn Assizes, commenting, 'I am one of those who consider that punishment should follow hard on the heels of guilt,' hastily adding that he was not expressing any opinion as to guilt or innocence. Barristers said their clients were ready to meet the charge 'now or at any time'. Apparently the two women expected to be acquitted, Catherine still firmly believing in the saving power of witchcraft.

What Peter Taylor expected is not known but at the pre-trial proceedings at the Autumn Assizes the Grand Jury, under the foremanship of Lord Walpole and on the direction of Mr Justice Bolland, discharged him. For all his elation, later to be horribly demonstrated, his day would come.

A grim place. The prisoners were
interrogated at the Walsingham Bridewell.
Peter Scholes

On 7 August 1835, Frances Billing and Catherine Frarey stood in the dock before Mr Justice Bolland. They pleaded 'Not Guilty' to charges of murdering Mary Taylor, Catherine as principal and Frances as accessory, and jointly murdering Robert Frarey. The courtroom was filled 'to suffocation', with standing room allowed.

The indictment and evidence naming Mary Taylor came first and witnesses spoke of things they had seen and heard, though not, as we shall see, in total worth. The identification of arsenic in the bodies was not disputed, just queried. The judge asked questions of Griffin to ascertain the means he had employed to identify the poison, and at the end said he was satisfied arsenic had been used. The evidence of the sale of the poison was indisputable. Eyewitness and circumstantial evidence pointed to how it had been used, and by whom.

The judge summed up and implored the jury 'to lay out of your minds all rumours that might have spread through the country.'

The jury quickly came to a verdict on the charge of murdering Mary Taylor: 'Guilty' against both women, Catherine as principal, Frances as accessory. Catherine had to be supported in the dock as she contemplated the awful consequences of that verdict, and the failure of the mystical powers she had relied upon. The women were then arraigned on the indictment naming Robert Frarey, jointly charged with his murder.

Elizabeth Southgate gave evidence of seeing powder in porter and Hannah Shorten (in custody for want of sureties) gave evidence of purchasing arsenic at the behest of Frances and with the knowledge of Catherine. Shorten denied she was a 'cunning woman', as alleged by the defence, but made a limited admission to fortune-telling. Catherine's gruel, tainted by the first verdict, became common to both deaths.

The verdict arrived within minutes: 'Guilty!' Catherine lapsed into hysterics, the atmosphere further stressed by shrieks from the public gallery. Frances stared blindly ahead.

Mr Justice Bolland began speaking in a solemn voice, faltering as

Catherine was held up in the dock crying, 'I am not guilty, my lord.' He continued, delivering his words with effort and visible emotion, telling the women they had been 'living a profligate, vicious and abandoned cause of life, and for the gratification of your lusts you hesitated not to make a sacrifice of human life.' He said, 'Against poison no person can be guarded.' Amid scenes of great emotion and despair, wearing the black cap, he finished, 'Your hours in this world are now numbered and few indeed those hours are.' He sentenced them to be hanged on 'Monday next at twelve o'clock', three days hence.'

Catherine Frarey was dragged screaming from the dock, her cries fading with distance. Frances Billing followed, stony-faced, without assistance. They knew they were dead women walking. *The Times* of London reported: 'No sympathy appeared to tell towards these monsters in human form on the part of the auditory.' The newspaper concluded: 'Thus ended an inquiry into one of the most atrocious deeds of violence ever perpetrated in this country.'

The heart-rending scenes at the Assizes were as nothing to those witnessed the next day, Saturday, at Norwich Castle as the children of the condemned women said their farewells. It was reported that two daughters of Frances Billing hung around her neck in 'speechless agony' and the anguish of both women and their children was terrible to behold. Catherine, in a frantic state, called to her murdered husband saying that she would soon appear before him.

James Billing saw his wife for the last time. She begged his forgiveness in a tearful scene in which she called herself 'a poor wretch of a wife'. He forgave her and poignantly said his farewell.

Outside Norwich Castle on Monday, 10 August, a crowd grew steadily throughout the morning, gathered in subdued and fearful expectancy, notably different to the boisterous assemblies that usually attended public executions. The *Norfolk Chronicle* reported: 'On no former occasion of a similar kind do we remember to have witnessed so great a multitude of spectators assembled.' There were other differences. In a last dreadful glimpse of chivalry the scaffold had been erected at the upper end of the bridge leading into the castle, to shorten the walk between prison gate and death. A murmuring crowd waited. Among them was Peter Taylor.

Two minutes before noon the prison gates opened and the women appeared amid the usual procession of prison governor, justices, surgeon and executioner, the chaplain leading the way intoning from the Book of Prayer. Catherine, wearing widow's weeds and cap, in evident distress, was dragged between two warders. Frances, wearing a coloured dress, walked steadily, staring ahead. The *Norfolk Chronicle* described 'a sight which no one but an alien to humanity could look upon unmoved.'

Events moved unhesitatingly. The chaplain read the funeral service as the women held hands, Frances helping Catherine up the scaffold steps. The executioner, William Calcraft, and his assistant, slipped white cloth

The confession of Frances Billing, in reality a blame-shifting attempt written on a scrap of paper by Thomas Readwin acting as parish clerk or constable. Norfolk Record Office

The final sentence of Billing's confession, on a separate piece of paper, absolves Peter Taylor. Her signature is well-written in an age when many could not write. Norfolk Record Office

bags over the women's heads and placed and adjusted nooses, next strapping their legs and positioning their feet. The crowd fell into hushed silence. There was a clatter and the women dropped. Screams came from the crowd, then silence. Frances died instantly, her neck broken. Catherine struggled, convulsing and choking to death. They remained suspended together for the customary hour and were later buried in the castle grounds.

The crowd slowly dispersed, but not before an altercation had taken place. Peter Taylor had expressed 'great satisfaction' with the executions, a statement that precipitated his identification and flight from Castle Hill.

Taylor escaped a wrathful crowd in Norwich but ran into trouble at his brother's cottage at Burnham Market. A crowd laid siege to the cottage and after windows had been broken he hid in a wardrobe. As fractious elements continued to swirl around the area he escaped from the back of the cottage, fleeing to his home parish of Whissonsett.

The case appeared to be over, consigned to history in all its horrific uniqueness. Peter Taylor had been saved by insufficient evidence. Those who could have convicted him were now dead; but then came news that shortly before death Frances and Catherine had been given 'to confession, supplication and prayer'. Frances had admitted 'criminal intercourse' with Peter Taylor, saying he had promised to marry her when

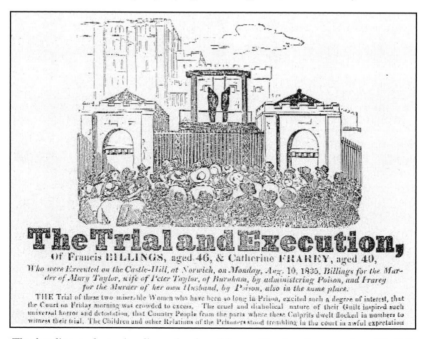

The heading and opening lines of a broadsheet sold after the executions. Norfolk Heritage Centre

they were both free. She said he had been aware of what was going on but had not taken an active part. She admitted mixing arsenic with the pills prescribed for Robert Frarey and, on four separate occasions, putting arsenic in his porter, also putting arsenic in gravy, flour and sugar in the Taylors' cottage.

Catherine confessed to putting arsenic in gruel for Mary Taylor and giving her own husband the poison in tea, porter and pills. She said she had attempted to poison her husband before she met Frances Billing. After they became friends she had agreed to 'remove James Billing by some means'.

Catherine's confession supposedly named 'partners to her guilt', but whatever she said, the shadowy and unsavoury Mr Gridley and the sinister Hannah Shorten slipped away into undeserved obscurity. Peter Taylor did not slip away.

Public opinion reviled Peter Taylor as a shiftless and unfaithful husband, a conspirator and accessory to murder, poisoner of a wife who had been well liked and had taken hours to die in agony. And two women had died on the scaffold protecting him, or so it seemed to many who were cognisant of gossip and careless of real evidence. And nobody liked a person deemed to have got away with murder.

Amid rumour, speculation and condemnation of Peter Taylor, witnesses spoke again, of matters not heard at the trial. Magistrates, driven by public furore, had Peter Taylor rearrested at Whissonsett. The original investigation had been less than thorough.

On 29 August magistrates took new depositions and committed Taylor in custody for trial as an accessory before the fact to his wife's murder. This time the Grand Jury, again under the foremanship of Lord Walpole, found a true bill.

The trial, before Mr Justice Gaselee, in April 1836, now produced the full observations and remarks overheard by Elizabeth Southgate and Edward Sparks. These bombshells of evidence, inexplicably missed in original depositions, drew the expected response from defending counsel, Mr O'Malley. He tried to show Southgate as dishonest or at best muddled in her recollections. He asked why she had not given this evidence before and she replied that she had not been asked. She said that all the questions put to her had been about Robert Frarey. Mr O'Malley cross-examined to no avail. She was unwavering in her simplicity; she knew what she had seen and heard and she had not previously been asked about it.

Southgate's explanation of docility under interview by magistrates does not sit easily with her previous alert, inquisitive behaviour. Surely she would blurt out everything she knew at the first opportunity. Not necessarily. She was illiterate, humble, a woman of her time and place, in awe of and giving stilted replies to questions from magistrates who

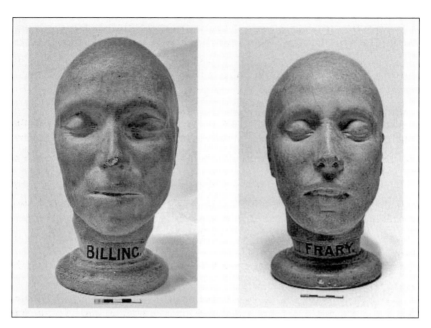

The death masks of Billing and Frarey. After hanging for one hour they were cut down, their heads were shaved and casts taken of their features, pursuing the belief of the time that phrenology would reveal a criminal disposition. Norfolk Museums & Archaeology Services

were careless of the wider picture. These were forelock-tugging, speak-when-spoken-to days.

One witness producing belated and startling evidence might have been channelled into a backwater of doubt by the defence, but they had to meet Sparks's evidence of Taylor saying to Frances, 'Never mind, she will soon be done away with and it will be alright with us.' If that remark, combined with Southgate's evidence of Taylor handing over a packet and saying 'That's enough for her,' was believed, then it was all over for Taylor.

Did brother and sister, for whatever reason, invent their evidence or tell it as they saw and heard it, but only when asked? There is a lesson here for all professional interviewers.

Mr O'Malley sought to show Sparks as a worthless individual giving evidence undeserving of consideration. He claimed that Sparks had been dismissed from his job as a mail cart driver after letters had disappeared. Sparks replied that he had been dismissed for carrying passengers. Sparks was without doubt unreliable and not the brightest of individuals, but his evidence, like his sister's, remained for the jury to believe or disbelieve.

James Billing gave evidence of his late wife's affair with Peter Taylor, particularly the hole-in-the-wall conversation, including the damning remark from Frances, 'Another Sunday will finish our concern.'

Phoebe Taylor gave evidence for the defence, saying the flour used by her brother-in-law had been good and he had been taken ill at the same time as his wife. Cross-examination revealed she had not observed his illness, merely been told by him; the judge discounted this hearsay evidence.

Peter Taylor spoke on his own behalf, denying all that told against him and asserting that he had genuinely been ill at the same time as his wife. He said he had insisted on the doctor being called to her and he did not know what arsenic was.

The judge reviewed the facts and advised the jury that judgement of the evidence and the persons giving it was for them. They were not long in deliberation, finding Taylor guilty, as charged.

Mr Justice Gaselee sentenced Taylor to death and told him he could expect little hope of mercy. The verdict and sentence brought approval from the *Norfolk Chronicle*, which described Taylor's defence as 'utterly unworthy of credit'.

On Saturday, 23 April 1836, at Norwich Castle at twelve noon, Peter Taylor, protesting his innocence to the last, met the same fate as his lover. The *Norfolk Chronicle* reported that he was 'led forth in a state of greatest prostration'. Shabbily dressed and trembling, he was lifted to the scaffold by two warders before a crowd of thousands. The *Norfolk Chronicle* has the last word: 'With more than the usual rapidity the profligate instigator of a most atrocious crime underwent the justly doomed and awful sentence of the law.'

Burnham Market, stained by murderers, ironically originating from other parishes, returned to normal community life with the traditional resolve of country folk. The three cottages of infamy became hard to let because they were reputedly haunted, a not unusual assertion after murder has been committed. They became known as 'Murderers' Row' and 'Poisoners' Piece'. Now they have gone, as have all who were there. But history does not go away and the record of something horrible remains for all time, recalled more than once by the thespians of this peaceful village re-enacting the murders in a stage play, to full houses, the last in 2003. They have raised over £1000 for the local church. Two centuries on, good comes from bad.

CHAPTER 4

The New Police

Murder of the Denver Fortune-Teller, 1837

Some nineteenth-century murders are well documented and have been retold over the years in varying detail. Strangely, one of the most remarkable has remained largely unknown, yet it is a milestone in early policing and an outstanding example of travelling criminals when travel required either a horse or stamina and strong footwear. It is also a tale of savagery, idiocy and endurance by villains, matched by initiative, determination and detection by citizens. It deserves to be recognised within the early days of professional and neighbourhood policing.

Norfolk welcomed its first professional police in 1836, though the welcome was not, of course, unanimous and the county as a whole missed out until 1839 (effectively January 1840). The inhabitants of Norwich, Great Yarmouth, Thetford and King's Lynn got their own police forces, a result of the Municipal Corporations Act, 1835 pushing town and city councils into something they had been procrastinating about for several years. The Rural Constabulary Act, 1839 did the same for county justices.

The few hundred inhabitants of Denver, a village in West Norfolk, knew little of this evolution of policing and probably cared less. They were situated one and a half miles from the small town of Downham Market and thirteen from the larger town of King's Lynn, served or supervised, depending upon your viewpoint and station in life, by the long-nurtured system of parish constables doing the bidding of magistrates and others of position and power. Hannah Manfield lived in Denver, in a half cottage opposite rough common land, and in 1837 she captured the attention of the police, old and new. She did so by dying, suddenly and brutally.

Hannah Manfield was believed to be around seventy years of age when she died, living alone and thought to be a spinster. She had lived for twenty-nine years in her cottage and little was known of her life before then. Some knew her as Manfield or Mansfield, others knew her as Sadler. Her real name was going to prove important.

Hannah was a card-dealing fortune-teller in an age when fear, awe and strong beliefs attended the calling. Some, inevitably, would see her as a witch but many an anxious and hopeful face beat a path to her door. She was also a collector of silver and fine coins, some of which were on view in a buffet arrangement in her living room, which was also her card-reading room. She would not be the first or last to die for perceived isolation and wealth.

The New Year 1837 came in amid severe weather and a nationwide influenza epidemic but, in the late evening of 2 January, a three-inch layer of snow and freezing temperature did not deter Hannah from calling upon her immediate neighbour, Sarah Dungay. On this cold and ultimately tragic night Hannah returned home at half past eleven and Sarah stayed up until one in the morning, unaware of the menace that lurked outside waiting for her candle to go out.

At around two in the morning Sarah Dungay's husband, Moses, _awakened to 'a rumbling noise'. He went to the window, opened it, looked out, saw nothing and hastily retreated in the face of the bitter cold.

At ten-thirty that morning Ann Terrington, who lived with the Dungays, called at Hannah's cottage and noticed the front door had split against the bolt. She took her concern to Sarah Dungay. The two women returned to the door and noticed blood on the threshold, and blood spots in the snow. They pushed the door partly open, finding it stopped against a weight the other side. That weight was Hannah Manfield, lying face down in her nightdress and covered in blood.

Moses Dungay and other men drawn to the horrific scene turned the body over to reveal that the throat had been severed to a considerable depth. The body was cold and stiff.

Footprints in the snow showed that two persons had approached the cottage on one side of the footpath, using virgin snow to muffle their approach and careless of the impressions they were leaving. Moses Dungay covered the most distinctly formed footprint with a wash tub. Near the door, the blood spots in the snow were as if somebody had shaken bloodied hands (they had). Elsewhere in the yard there were bloodstains on straw and snow.

Henry Goss, an accountant from Downham Market, went to the scene in the role of parish constable. He tracked the footprints to the nearby lane, at which point two persons had walked on opposite sides, possibly a third in the middle where the snow was impacted from other foot traffic. More footprints trailed across the common in the direction of the turnpike (Ely to Downham Market). Goss distinguished between the footprints by one set being larger than the others and 'nailed and peculiarly shaped', whilst another showed an unusual proficiency of nails. He sketched the multi-nailed print. More footprints trailed round the Dungays' cottage, repeated alongside a bordering hedge. Two hedge-securing stakes had been pulled from the ground and were missing.

John Long, a parish constable from Downham Market, found dirty footprints inside Hannah's cottage that did not correspond with those

The joined cottages in 1900. The Dungays lived nearest the gate, Hannah Manfield at the far end. Edna Sharpe

outside. Conclusions were of burglary and murder by three men, and there had been a circling reconnaissance of the cottages.

Thomas Wales, a surgeon from Downham Market, examined the body. He concluded a knife had been thrust into the throat 'with great violence' and 'the first thrust had perforated the cartilage of the second joint of the neck', causing death. He thought the weapon to be a 'strong, pointed, locked knife' and that after the initial thrust it had been drawn across the throat.

Philip Beeton, a millwright from Denver, one of several drawn to the scene with mixed feelings of community spirit, curiosity and morbidity, stepped over the body and went inside the cottage to discover Hannah's clothes lying on a table with the pockets rifled. Items of silver lay nearby, seemingly the residue of a frenzied and abandoned search; they comprised a jug, salt cellar and odd spoon, and 'seven sovereigns, three half-sovereigns and a half-guinea as bright as when they were first made', also 'about a pound's worth of silver'. Inside an unlocked cupboard he found silver plate. Had the intruders been disturbed by Hannah and in panic killed her and fled? The truth would be more cold-blooded.

The crime had the hallmarks of rough-and-ready villains with failed nerves, probably men of low intellect with criminal records. In a sparsely populated countryside, in the depths of winter, the murderers had possibly drawn attention to themselves before the crime and after. Such was the case.

A quickly convened inquest heard evidence of the discovery of the body, the injuries, footprints and apparently missing silver. The jury returned a verdict of murder by persons unknown.

Public concern swiftly reached high places, aided by a postal system seemingly superior to that of two centuries later. On 4 January, Home Secretary Lord John Russell wrote to Edward Lett, Clerk to Downham Market magistrates, asking how the case was progressing. His interest so soon can only have been instigated by somebody in a high position in the county, somebody aware that he would see the circumstances as a test of the new order of policing, except Denver was not located within any of the new policing jurisdictions. Mr Lett replied on 5 January, giving the inquest jury's verdict and concluding, 'The case seems as involved a mystery such as we have no clue to find out the offenders' – hardly a reply to enthuse a government promoting new law and order.

Mr Lett's admission of bafflement spurred new action. An officer of the new King's Lynn force was assigned to the case. Thomas Valentine Wright, a shoemaker by trade and a Sergeant at Mace in the town, had joined the new force on its inception on 25 January 1836 as a day constable. Now he would be the flag-bearer of a new age of policing, investigating a murder outside his normal jurisdiction.

In later times, trained police would investigate murder with dedicated systems that trawled for and analysed information, calling upon a back-up of increasingly sophisticated technology and forensic aids.

A murder discovered, sketched from deposition descriptions. David Rowlands

Constable Wright knew only about shoes, coincidentally to be an asset in this case. He had no understanding of the 'principle of exchange', which allied a crime scene to a suspect, nor would he have the use of finger-prints, photography, dedicated pathology, scientific analysis and medical expertise that grouped and matched blood. Neither would he have com-munications that joined police forces and appealed to and fuelled the public's sense of outrage. But Constable Wright did have an observant public: stories emerged of three men walking along freezing country roads at night.

On New Year's Day three men had sought refuge from the chilling cold in *The Bell* public house at Southery, a village five miles to the south of Denver. They were roughly dressed and said they were bankers (dug ditches and banked the earth) and navigators (worked on canals and rail-ways). They stayed the night at *The Bell*.

The men left the public house a little after five o'clock on the evening of Monday, 2 January, walking towards Denver. They made a strong-looking group, one six feet tall and powerfully built, another shorter, broader and athletic-looking, and the third tall and slender with long, dark hair. The broad, athletic one limped. He had spoken of a knee sore from walking.

On a bitterly cold moonlit night, between seven and eight o'clock, the men came up behind Robert Wilson walking the same road. They engaged him in conversation and walked 'better than a mile' with him, asking about the villages that lay ahead. The big man asked Wilson if he had a watch and when Wilson said he hadn't he showed him a silver pocket watch, ensuring he would be remembered.

John Barton, landlord of the *George and Dragon* public house at Hilgay, two miles from Denver, would be the last to see the three men before Hannah Manfield. Publicans traditionally have a practised eye and memory for anything or anybody not seen before, especially in open countryside. The men arrived between seven and eight o'clock and stayed drinking until eleven. Barton noticed that the biggest man had a strap round his wrist.

None of the three were from Norfolk, though two were near enough and one of these would be known to some of the persons he met that night. John Smith (as he was known to this case) had some local knowl-edge and that made him the prime mover in the night's deadly plan. His real name was John Day and he was twenty-five years of age, a man with convictions for theft and violence. He came from near Boston in Lincolnshire and he wore a strap around his wrist. Tall and strong-looking, he was, however, seriously ill, suffering from consumption.

George Timms, aged twenty-two years, the shorter, widely built one, had a criminal history, notably as a poacher. He came from Whittlesea (Whittlesey) in Cambridgeshire and his local knowledge would have its place in the odyssey to follow. He dragged his sore knee in poor temper and, with Smith, was more expressive and volatile than the third man, John Varnham.

Documents give different spellings of Varnham and all are wrong: his real name was William Maskell. Varnham, as he is known to this case, was twenty-five years of age and came from a respectable family living near Brighton. His father was a shepherd. Varnham had left home to follow public works employments and whilst he was a participating voice in the threesome he was more the follower. The agreed objective of the men was Hannah Manfield. And they had walked from London to realise it.

The next sighting of Smith, Timms and Varnham, apart from that of somebody who would never speak again, came from William Tooke, a Downham Market chimney sweep on his way to work with 'his boy'. At three o'clock (Tooke heard a church clock striking), in the bitter cold of the morning of Tuesday, 3 January, he saw three men walking quickly through Denver towards Downham Market, less than a mile from Hannah Manfield's cottage. He passed them in the opposite direction without speaking but noted enough to accurately describe them. His boy, Daniel Carle, was even more perceptive. He saw that one of the men was carrying a hedge stake.

The three men trudged into Cambridgeshire and were seen at Parson Drove by Richard Goodyear, another consigned to night work by the nature of his trade – driving the night-soil cart. He recognised John Smith as John Day and called out, 'Well, old mates, you have had a long journey of it tonight.' Varnham shouted back that he was tired and jumped onto the cart (not the nicest transport to hitch a lift upon) and Smith and Timms followed him.

At eight o'clock that morning Goodyear's cart and passengers met the night-soil cart of John Coats on the Leverington road near Wisbech. Coats noted that Goodyear's passengers had rime-encrusted whiskers and deduced they had been out all night. Recognising Smith as John Day, he called out and received abuse in return, ensuring he also would remember them.

The men moved into Lincolnshire on foot and began adding to the potential witness tally. Benjamin Bunn kept *The White Horse* at Sutton St Edmund and saw the three men arrive at about eleven o'clock in the morning. They were tired and cold, and probably not smelling too well. They paid for their drink with a bright new sixpence, the coin attracting the attention of the landlord. The men said it was a new coin and they had got it from Lisbon, a story guaranteed to be locked into the landlord's memory.

To compound their foolishness Smith took back the sixpence saying, 'You don't think it's a good one,' and replacing it with a similarly bright shilling.

Robert and Sarah Hurst were keepers of *The Duke's Head* at Whaplode Drove, another drinking and rest station for the men who

Murderers on the road, sketched from deposition descriptions. David Rowlands

arrived at around six o'clock on the Tuesday evening and stayed until the Friday morning. The Hursts knew Smith and heard the others referred to as George and Jack. George Timms wore stockings that were dirty and wet to the knees and Mrs Hurst learned from the men's conversation that Smith had pushed him into a dyke. Mrs Hurst's twelve-year-old daughter was given the task of washing the stockings.

Timms sought to replace rapidly shredding boots and asked in the public house if anyone knew a shoemaker. William Clayton stepped forward and said he could make Timms two pairs of boots by next morning. Varnham asked for a pair of half-boots and Clayton supplied him with a ready-made pair.

As Varnham bent forward to remove his boots a handkerchief fell from his pocket, spilling out silver spoons. He grabbed them and returned them to his pocket. Nobody said anything but the silence was heavy with implication.

Varnham cut the tops off his old boots and threw them onto the pub fire. He left the bottoms and Mrs Hurst threw them on the fire. She kept the metal cleats.

The next morning Timms collected his new boots from Clayton's shop in Whaplode Drove and advised the shoemaker not to talk about the falling spoons. He said they had got them from Lisbon, adding, 'My fool of a mate got fresh one night and slipped them off the table.'

Clayton said it made no odds to him and received payment of a half-sovereign, a shilling and a sixpence. For the second pair of boots Timms paid him a half-guinea.

The trail, now littered with evidence and witnesses, moved back into Cambridgeshire and to Timms's home territory of Whittlesea, where the men acquired new velveteen jackets with pearl buttons. Timms left his old coat with his uncle, a careful move that was to be undone when the uncle handed it to Timms's mother – the first person the police would visit.

On Saturday, 7 January, Timms met George Byatt, a local gunsmith, in *The Black Bull* public house and said he had some silver to sell and he would take a pair of pogs (pistols) for some of it. The following night Byatt saw all three men and the silver, produced in a lump weighed at two pounds and two ounces. He asked why it was in a lump and Smith said it would not do to carry it about without melting it first, a remark steeped in significance. Smith said they had done the melting in an iron saucepan and originally the silver had comprised salts, tea and table-spoons. That Byatt didn't supply the pistols possibly owed something to an inbuilt caution combined with a perception that Timms was the kind of man to blaze a trail back to him.

Byatt asked where the silver had come from and received the reply: 'On the railroad a hundred miles off.' Byatt said the next-door watch-maker might purchase the silver and Timms asked him to broker a deal. That night the silver stayed with Byatt and he cut it into seven unequal pieces.

On the Monday morning, 9 January, Smith called upon Byatt and was informed that the watchmaker would not buy the silver. That after-noon Byatt met the three men in *The Black Bull*, Timms now accompanied by his father, and they said they would call for the silver the next morning.

At Byatt's house next morning, Smith produced three keys and asked Byatt if they were of any use to him. When the gunsmith declared he was not interested Smith threw the keys to Mrs Byatt and she put them on a ring already loaded with keys. She asked if they [she and her husband] might have some silver for their trouble and Smith handed over a small piece. He offered a silver pocket watch, as seen by Robert Wilson, saying he had got it from his landlord, which was true. He had stolen it. The watch would later introduce an element of confusion because it had not belonged to Hannah Manfield. Mrs Byatt purchased it for fifteen shillings.

The three villains left Whittlesea and turned north. At Stamford they sold a silver cup to a Mr Brooks. Again, this had not belonged to Hannah Manfield.

Reaching Doncaster at midnight on Thursday night, they stayed at a disreputable hostelry called *The Bird in Hand*. The next day, 13 January, they appeared at, of all places, the West Riding Sessions, where they sat for most of the day in the public gallery watching the dispensation of northern justice. Were they interested in a specific case or were they, fresh from committing murder, motivated by feelings of defiance and superiority? Distance made for safety, they thought.

In an age when communication and transport were basic, the three self-assured men could not have known that the new police were behind them, and catching up. Witnesses had spoken, descriptions and names had been noted, a direction of travel assessed. Police Constable Wright had traced their progress from Ely, two days before the murder, to Southery and Hilgay and beyond Denver to Whaplode Drove. He set out in pursuit with Parish Constable Long, using the coach service, but at Spalding Long fell victim to the influenza epidemic and Wright pressed on alone. He knew one of the men was John Day, known to be big and violent, and the others were called George and Jack. He did not know that Day and George had sworn they would not be taken alive.

At Stamford, Wright learned his quarry had continued northwards and he followed to Grantham, Wakefield and Doncaster, searching as he went. The *Norfolk Chronicle* was to describe him as 'a very active police officer ... indefatigable in endeavouring to discover the perpetrators.'

Wright arrived in Doncaster in the early morning of Saturday, 14 January, by express coach. He began searching the town, obtaining assistance from Chief Constable Thomas Tymms of the new Doncaster Borough Police, possibly the first instance of co-operation between distant police forces in a murder case.

At eleven that morning Wright saw a man he was sure was John Day carrying a loaf of bread. He followed him to *The Bird in Hand* and saw his other targets lolling inside. Beef steaks were cooking on a stove. This relaxing scene shattered into startled exclamations as, with the element of surprise, policemen charged into the room and pinioned the three men. The speed and effectiveness of the arrests can be set against Smith's and Timms's assertions they would never be taken alive.

Smith had in his possession three sovereigns, fourteen shillings in silver, a picklock, some rope and a large bone-handled knife with blood on the handle. He was wearing a slop (roughly made waistcoat) with washed blood on the breast. He said he had been working in London and did not know where he had been since.

Timms was in possession of a wedge of melted silver wrapped in a rag and had a bundle which contained a slop stained with washed blood. He also had a knife. He said he had been working in London and had left in the company of the other two.

Varnham had two knives and wore a slop that showed blood spots. He said he had been in London with Timms and had bought his new boots in Paddington. He claimed he had met Smith on the road to Birmingham.

All the men said they had not been to Norfolk.

The prisoners' hands and feet were shackled before they began the drawn-out, jolting coach journey back to Norfolk, a journey not without incident. Stopping at Newark to change horses and refresh, the prisoners made a shuffling return to the coach in front of a growing crowd (news had travelled faster than the coach) and as Varnham mounted the coach steps he, in the words of the *Norfolk Chronicle*, 'pulled off his hat and huzzaed, which struck terror in the minds of hundreds of spectators.'

The arrested men were lodged in Swaffham Prison, from where they made several appearances before examining magistrates at Downham Market, denying ever being in the neighbourhood of the murder or even knowing that part of the country. Their claim that they did not know Hannah Manfield was refuted by Sarah and Mary Dungay, who gave evidence that nearly a year earlier three men had arrived at their cottage, one stepping forward and asking for advice, the other two staying in the background. Sarah Dungay guessed the man wanted his fortune told and asked her daughter to take him next door, where Hannah Manfield asked what he wanted.

The man said he wanted to speak 'about losses'. Hannah reluctantly let all three men into her cottage.

Sarah and Mary Dungay identified John Smith as the advice-seeking man. They were unsure about the others. If their identification was correct, and it would be disputed, Smith had spent nearly a year plotting the crime.

As more witnesses were traced and evidence mounted the prisoners went back and forth between gaol and magistrates. Henry Bellairs, a solicitor from Whittlesea, provided a damning piece of evidence. He took the bunch of keys from Mrs Byatt and travelled to Denver to show them to Sarah Dungay. She picked out three of the keys as familiar to her, one of which was broken. Bellairs fitted two of these familiar keys in Hannah Manfield's cottage, one to a small box and the other, the broken one, to a cupboard door.

The boot cleat left by Varnham, kept by Mrs Hurst, compared favourably with Goss's sketch of the footprint in the snow. A bright half-guinea that shoemaker Clayton had been slow to spend also appeared in evidence, along with the bloodstained knife taken from Smith. The prisoners' clothing provided more stained examples. Edward Pearson, a warder at Swaffham Prison, took Timms's breeches away when he saw they were marked with washed blood. In Whittlesea Constable Sadd seized a bloodstained coat from the mother of Timms. In all these cases blood was identified by opinion.

Positive identifications of the men in places they said they hadn't been may have owed something to the witnesses viewing them in custody in Downham Market, with the inevitable conclusion that the police had got the right men.

Examining magistrates did not find all the witnesses co-operative, including George Byatt, by now wishing he had never seen Timms and his mates. He prevaricated so much he was ordered to find sureties to appear in 'the after-stage of the proceedings' or be committed to custody. He reluctantly admitted selling the piece of silver received from Smith 'to a Jew at Wisbech,' identified as Antonio Montegani – who subsequently gave up the silver.

Mr Brooks at Stamford, purchaser of the silver cup, was just as difficult. He had been cautioned not to part with the cup pending his appearance before the magistrates but when he did appear he said he had sold it to 'a travelling Jew.' The magistrates placed him in the custody of a constable to travel back to Stamford and find the silver or the Jew, failing which he would be committed to Norwich Castle. There the record ceases. Mr Brook disappears from the case. Perhaps the magistrates discovered his purchase did not relate to Hannah Manfield, or perhaps he really disappeared. The three prisoners were committed to the Norfolk Assizes.

On 6 April 1837, John Smith, alias Day, George Timms and John Varnham, alias William Maskell, appeared at the Norfolk Assizes in Norwich before Mr Justice Coltman. They pleaded 'Not Guilty' to murder and the trial began with arguments over who had been murdered.

Mr Prendergast and Mr O'Malley appeared for the prosecution and were taken unawares when defending counsel, Mr Gunning and Mr

The heading of a graphic broadsheet issued after the arrests, presuming the guilt of the arrested men and getting wrong the names of the victim and one of the accused. Norfolk Heritage Centre

Dasent, cross-examined witnesses as to Hannah Manfield's real name, submitting that it was Sadler and therefore the indictment was wrong and their clients could not answer to it. (Some reports called her Mansfield).

Sarah Dungay said Hannah had told her that her name was Hannah Sadler Manfield. Sarah believed Sadler was the name of Hannah's mother and her father was named Manfield, and she had been born out of wedlock and never married.

Mr O'Malley argued that Manfield was her common name. Mr Gunning said that wasn't enough, she had to be identified by her real name. The judge favoured Mr Gunning's view but retired to consult his fellow judge. He returned to say he would reserve the point and in the meantime he would allow the case to proceed. (Records show that John Manfield, farmer, married Hannah Sadler in 1787 at Denver and died at Denver in 1795).

Evidence of finding the body, during which Smith fainted – apparently from his illness, led to surgeon Thomas Wales giving his opinion that the stains on the prisoners' clothing were blood. He said that Smith's slop was heavily stained. He thought that Smith's knife could have caused the fatal wound and the stains on its handle were definitely blood. Questioned by the defence, he had to admit he could not tell if the blood was human or animal.

Timms trembled and became agitated during Wales's evidence and Smith was now clearly very ill. He was allowed to sit in the dock.

Constable Long had compared Henry Goss's sketched footprint with Varnham's boot cleat and found they matched. That evidence lost its value when he was cross-examined and admitted he had made some alterations to Goss's sketch. Mr Gunning immediately objected to the sketch and cleat as evidence and the judge directed that the jury should not have sight of either.

Goss was questioned in depth about the number of nails shown by the footprint in the snow, and though he gave his evidence stoutly the jury, without the sketch and cleat, must have been left with a kaleidoscopic recall of nailed boots. The initiative over footprints at the scene had not been properly collated and adequately presented, and had been easily diverted by the defence – though they decided not to question Constable Wright on footwear when they discovered he was a shoemaker by trade. William Clayton identified the new boots he had sold to Timms and Varnham.

Evidence of keys that fitted inside Hannah Manfield's cottage did not impress the defence. They cross-examined Henry Bellairs and established that he had not tried the keys to see if they fitted in other property.

As well as the defence might be doing in the face of crushing evidence they were confounded by witnesses more used to being defendants. William Parker came from Denver and was in Swaffham Prison for assaulting a constable. While he was there Smith asked him if he had heard of the murder and Parker, who had been one of the many to view the body, said he had. Smith asked how the woman had been cut and Parker said 'from ear to ear'. Smith said they had 'meant to do the old bugger' and described how he had gone 'with two mates' across 'some bloody old common' and 'the bloody old furze pricked my legs.' Cross-examined, Parker said he was not aware a reward had been offered for information.

George Hassock, in Swaffham Prison for riotous conduct, knew Smith and asked him if anyone had seen him near the murder. Smith said he didn't think so, adding that he went to the woman's house and 'called her up' but 'the old bugger' refused to come down. He told Hassock, 'If you see my mates tell them to hold their own.' In cross-examination Hassock said he had been in gaol about five times. He also had not heard of a reward, he said.

John Neave, in Swaffham Prison for disorderly conduct and assaulting a constable, said Smith conversed with him, Parker and Hassock 'whilst other prisoners were gone to the wheel'. Smith had told him of crossing the common and also said if he had known the constables were coming they would not have had him.

Charles Benson, in Swaffham Prison for not maintaining his family, spoke to Varnham while sweeping the passage outside his cell. Varnham said that if his mates held their own they would be alright, adding that 'if they [the prosecution] could not tell a better tale than they had told they could do nothing with them.'

Mr Gunning and Mr Dasent consistently plugged the vagueness of the victim's identity and Mr Gunning concluded by saying that the evidence against his clients was full of discrepancies and he would not call any witnesses – another way of saying he didn't have any.

The judge summed up for nearly two hours and said he would allow the question of the victim's identity to go to the jury. The jury deliberated for a quarter of an hour and returned a verdict of 'Guilty' against all three accused, adding that they found the deceased to have been Hannah Sadler, having acquired the name of Hannah Manfield by reputation (a false premise; as Denver marriage records would have shown). The jury's rider caused the judge to decline to pass sentence. At nearly one o'clock in the morning he adjourned the court.

At nine o'clock on the morning of 7 April three convicted murderers faced their nemesis. Mr Justice Coltman had consulted with Mr Justice Parke overnight. He told the prisoners:

> A point of law has been urged in your favour, but not in any way affecting the intrinsic merits of the case, but of mere matter of form only. But as I intend to consult the other judges of the land upon it, sometime will necessarily elapse before your sentence will

necessarily be carried into execution. I warn you, however, not to entertain definitive hopes, for my decided opinion is that the point which is so reserved cannot possibly be of any avail to you.

He referred to a 'barbarous murder of a poor, aged, defenceless woman' and told them 'your early career is drawing to a close' and 'I earnestly entreat you to prepare to meet your heavenly judge.' He sentenced them to death.

Timms called in an agitated voice, 'If we cannot catch mercy here we can in another world.'

Smith, standing with difficulty, had a different concern, a surprising one in view of the sentence. He said, 'I hope that the clothes which have been taken from us will be delivered to us; there are a lot of silk handkerchiefs and other things which have not been produced.'

The judge replied, 'You will have all due attention paid to you.' This was inevitably true.

Incarcerated in Norwich Castle awaiting the end of their lives, the

The route to murder, over snow and rough ground at night. The common, viewed in better weather from outside the cottages in 2006. Author

three men confessed, Smith in some detail, his companions seemingly less so and more in the manner of 'alright I did it', all seeking the forgiveness of the Almighty. Confessing is, of course, not quite the same as telling the whole truth and, in the absence of official statements released for public consumption, what the men said fell to the mercy of scribes who professed to have 'authentic sources'. Newspapers and broadsheet publishers were never deterred by gaps in information and the latter were particularly inclined to realms of fantasy to spice and fill out their story. From published accounts, research and corroborative evidence the reader may take the following as the men's own account of their appalling crime, mainly told by Smith.

The plot had originated, Smith said, from time he had spent in hospital at Downham Market in early 1836, where he heard of the fortune-teller's reputed wealth. He said he acquired geographical pointers to the cottage and formed the intention to rob the fortune-teller. At this point accounts of Smith's confession differ. One version is that he admitted visiting Hannah Manfield's cottage on his release from hospital, as described by the Dungays, and in another he denied it and said that he immediately obtained work on the new railway in Hertfordshire, where he met Timms and Varnham. Certainly, together, in Hertfordshire, the three men savoured the retold stories of Hannah Manfield's silver. Together they plotted to acquire that silver.

After Smith had stolen silver, money and a watch by picking the lock of his landlord's room in Hertfordshire, they walked to London and there sold some of the stolen silver. An arrangement to meet 'a brother banker', who would join them and provide a brace of pistols, fell through when the brother banker did not turn up. Undeterred, the three men began walking to Denver. They quarrelled as they walked. Smith thought Hannah would have to be killed. Timms and Varnham wavered. Eventually and hesitantly the two doubters agreed that if she tried to raise the alarm whoever was nearest should silence her, for ever. They resumed their journey, drinking and arguing.

Twice on the journey they split up; once, Smith, despising his companions, trudged on alone vowing 'to do the job' single-handed. At Littleport in Cambridgeshire, after they had come together again, Varnham refused to take any further part and remained behind. He later caught them up.

Arriving at Denver via Ely, Southery and Hilgay they huddled in St Mary's churchyard in the bitter cold, cursing and reappraising their route. Smith, the leader and guide, had overshot the common he intended should bring them out in front of Hannah Manfield's cottage. They retraced their steps, found the common and, guided by distant lights, fought their way through snow and undergrowth to the cottages, where Timms and Varnham had second thoughts and were for calling the whole thing off. The joined cottages were larger than expected and lights were showing. Smith, however, insisted they had come too far to turn away. Again he said he would do it alone. Three men wandered the perimeter of the cottages swigging from a bottle of rum, one determined, two beset with misgivings. When the Dungays' light went out they hesitated, talked and decided.

At half past one in the morning they fastened the Dungays' doors with hedge stakes and attempted to break a window in Hannah Manfield's cottage. The noise brought Hannah to an upstairs window. Smith called upon her to open up, saying they had lost their way and needed directions. She told them to go away and called to her neighbours for help. Alarmed by her cries, the men forced the door and seized her as she came downstairs. She struggled and was thrown against the door by Smith and Timms. Varnham lit a candle and began searching.

As Hannah lay by the door, pleading for mercy, a most horrific act took place, freely admitted by Smith without variance from his confessing accomplices. Smith and Timms, in spoken agreement, snapped the poor woman's head back and, using Smith's knife, stabbed and slashed open her throat as a slaughterer would dispatch an animal, dropping her blood-spouting body to the floor. Such was the perceived horror of this act all three men fled from the cottage, stepping through the blood gushing across the doorway, clutching their quickly gathered booty. They made their way back to St Mary's churchyard, reappraised their shocking crime and, still arguing, set out on the road again.

Amazingly, all three men insisted that the blood found on their clothes did not relate to the murder but to fighting elsewhere. Techniques far into the future would have shown the truth. Smith and Timms admitted they had washed their bloodied hands in the snow outside. Varnham admitted he had trodden in the spreading pool of blood in his haste to leave.

Smith said that, on the road near Wisbech, Varnham collapsed weeping onto the verge and Timms trembled so much Smith contemptuously said he wished he had carried out the crime alone. The day after the killing Timms asked for a knife to cut his food and Smith gave him the murder weapon. Timms recoiled and Smith mocked him for his squeamishness. The men admitted that, in addition to the silver, they had got away with twenty or thirty pounds in sovereigns, guineas and other coins.

Awaiting execution all three men 'sought their peace with God', a new experience for Smith and Timms, who were reviled by the press and public for lives of 'idleness, refractory disposition, drinking, gambling, improvidence, debauchery and bad company of both sexes' – as one letter writer to the *Norwich Mercury* put it.

Timms's parents saw their son for the last time (his father had recently been acquitted of sheep stealing) following which the condemned man broke down. After they had left he wrote them a long farewell letter in which he said, 'I confess my guilt and own the justice of my sentence, and that I richly deserve to die. How bitterly do I regret my misspent time.'

Smith, by now referred to as Day in relevant documents, declared that he had 'by advice and persuasion' led Timms and Varnham into crime. As his health declined he was moved into the chaplain's room in the prison. There was a possibility he would cheat the gallows.

Varnham resigned himself to death by taking the sacrament. Execution was set for Saturday, 22 April, but this proved to be a false start, or false finish if you were awaiting death, and it caught out a Norwich broadsheet publisher who wrote that the condemned men appeared at the scaffold 'perfectly resigned' and 'Smith with difficulty ascended the fatal drop' and, at the hanging, 'a universal tremor agitated the mind of all present'. There was more in a similar vein, taking an avid reader through the whole dramatic proceedings of judicial death. But the executions had been postponed. Imaginative journalism had been caught out; the men were still alive. Were the judges still debating a name issue?

On the Thursday, two days before the new execution date of 29 April, Varnham heard that he had been reprieved. He fell to his knees, tipping his face to the ground with such force his nose bled. Transportation and

St Mary's churchyard, where the killers conferred before and after the murder, and where their victim lies (arrowed). Her headstone reads: 'Sacred to the Memory of Hannah Sadler Manfield who was most barbarously murdered by three bankers on 3rd January 1837.' Author

'perpetual confinement' would be his fate. Smith, learning of Varnham's reprieve, expressed his satisfaction.

On Saturday, 29 April 1837, John Smith, alias Day, and George Timms died on the gallows outside Norwich Castle watched by thousands. Timms walked to his death with, according to the *Norfolk Chronicle*, 'a slow and staggering step, hanging down his head and weeping bitterly.' The newspaper reported:

> Smith, alias Day, followed ... dressed in a blue smock ... a woollen cap on his head ... his countenance displayed a ghastly lividness of hue ... his expressive face tranquil ... his manner that of firmness and resignation.

Smith had to be helped up the steps to the gallows, as forecast by an impulsive publisher, and there he gazed around and said, 'What a number of people'. The executioner spent 'some minutes' placing and adjusting nooses during which Smith and Timms turned to face the castle, their lips moving silently. The bolt was withdrawn and they dropped, struggled and died. Justice of the time had come to Hannah Manfield lying in a Denver churchyard.

The bodies remained hanging for the customary hour following which they were laid in the yard of the castle and the prisoners, presumably including Varnham, were walked past. Smith and Timms were buried in the prison grounds.

The church often seized upon murders to demonstrate the fate of the unfaithful that went astray. At Bexwell, an adjunct of Downham Market and Denver, 700 persons struggled to get into a church to hear a sermon on the inevitable fate of murderers, given with 'thrilling effect' according to the *Norfolk Chronicle*.

Somewhere in the aftermath of this brutal murder there should be praise for the pursuit of justice by rural communities and the determination of a new police force. Thomas Valentine Wright, shoemaker and policeman, had set down a marker for the years to come. He went on to become Inspector of Weights and Measures and High Bailiff at King's Lynn.

CHAPTER 5

The New Police

The Murder of a Secret Wife, 1840

A shriek rent the night air, carrying over a still countryside, cutting off into stunning silence. The cry, a little before one o'clock on the morning of 18 June 1840, heralded tragedy and would be the prelude to revelations of deceit, greed and callousness, and of perverseness and opposition to inexorable justice. Death and scandal loomed in the purely rural setting of farms, cottages, fields and narrow lanes that comprise and surround Thwaite (Thwaite St Mary), aptly described in *White's 1845 Norfolk* as 'a picturesque dell, 12 miles S S E of Norwich, a parish of 110 souls and 667 acres of land', a description that survives today.

William Stowards lay awake in his farmhouse, disturbed by the cry. As a 25-year-old farmer he knew the sound of a schreech-owl and this was not one, a view reinforced by his lodger and brother-in-law, John Barnaby, calling from the next room to ask if he had heard the cry. Stowards called back that he had heard. Mrs Stowards sat up in bed and made the enquiry in both men's minds.

She said, 'Sure there is nothing the matter with poor Mary?'

Her husband and John Barnaby dressed and hurried the 300 yards to the farmhouse of 61-year-old James Barnaby, father of John, Mrs Stowards and 'poor Mary'. In the Barnaby parlour a candle glimmered near the point of extinction but there was no movement and the door of the wash-house, which connected to the kitchen, was open. Stowards knew that James Barnaby and his resident labourer, George Kent, aged seventeen years, had retired for the night because he had visited earlier, talking with Mary Barnaby as she sat sewing in the kitchen. He had left her at a quarter past eleven. By sight and sound she was no longer in the farmhouse.

Stowards and John Barnaby began a fearful search of the surrounding area, conscious of ongoing family troubles. James Barnaby had recently ordered his son and daughter, who was also his housekeeper, from the family home. John had left on the previous Sunday to lodge with the Stowards and Mary was to follow him that very day, the Friday, when a new housekeeper took up duties. Her possessions, including items of furniture, were ready for removal. This family displacement had resulted from the earlier arrest of James Barnaby, charged by John and Mary Barnaby with the attempted murder of Mary.

The attempt upon Mary's life had come through the favourite weapon of the age: arsenic. A quantity of the readily available powder had been placed overnight in the tea-kettle in James Barnaby's kitchen, seemingly aimed at Mary when, as housekeeper and early riser, she made her morning tea. The attempt failed because, on this occasion, she used the water in the kettle to mix the feed for their chickens and all nineteen died. James Barnaby was seen to be the only one with motive and opportunity and he spent four days in custody being interrogated by magistrates. His motive, as seen, was anger at the shame Mary was about to bring on her family. She could no longer disguise her pregnancy and as a 39-year-old single woman, disgrace and social stigma loomed.

Magistrates unconditionally released James Barnaby – the offer of bail from John Randalsome, a tenant farmer from Broome, was not required.

James Barnaby returned home in a rage and, in best Victorian fashion, ordered his son and daughter not to darken his doorstep again. Neither wanted to, fearing a further attempt on Mary's life. A frigid, non-speaking atmosphere prevailed pending departures.

John Barnaby had observed his sister's pregnancy and, after leaving home, learned from her the father's identity. He learned more than he bargained for. His sister was not a single woman. She had married John Randalsome at St Julian's Church, Norwich in April 1839 and Randalsome was the father, pursuing his relationship by regularly visiting her late at night. Armed with this information John Barnaby watched on Tuesday night, 16 June, and found Randalsome in the straw-house. The following night he again watched and this time he saw Mary going indoors through the wash-house and Randalsome leaving the straw-house. Now, the next night, he was searching for his sister without knowing that Mary had earlier told William Stowards she would be sitting up expecting John Randalsome to visit her.

Beset with knowledge and dread Barnaby and Stowards explored a stack-yard, outbuildings, the surrounding field and adjacent road. Barnaby went three times into the straw-house, motivated by his previous observations and unbelieving of his first two searches. Near two o'clock Stowards ventured fifty yards from the Barnaby farmhouse to the pond from which they drew their water and, under the gleam of moonlight, saw Mary Randalsome, née Barnaby, lying face down in the still water, her ruffled hair nearest the bank, her water-logged gown submerging the rest of her body into the shelving three-foot depth.

Stowards called John Barnaby and together they used a wooden stake that served as the pail holder for the pond, now uprooted and lying nearby, to hook Mary's clothing and tow her to the bank, heaving her onto dry ground. Barnaby roused men from nearby cottages and with the assistance of Henry Mitchell and John Balls they took her into the Barnaby farmhouse. James Barnaby and the boy, George Kent, were called from their beds and the boy dispatched to Bungay to inform surgeon Charles Garneys. Stowards struck out across fields to rouse Thomas Hindle, a farmer, and Thwaite's parish constable.

Hindle and Stowards hurried back around the field adjoining Barnaby's stack-yard, halting as the improving light of the near-shortest night of the year revealed footprints in the freshly ploughed earth. The prints led from near the gate by the stack-yard to a headland only a few yards from the pond, and back to the gate again, the return steps deep and well-spaced, indicative of a person running. Stowards drove a stake alongside a well-defined print.

News of the tragedy ran through homesteads and hamlets as folk rose early to work the land. Carter Parkerson maintained a farm at Broome and at just after five o'clock that morning he hailed Richard Randalsome as he arrived for work.

'Where was your brother last night?' Parkerson called from his window, the question significant in the asking. Without waiting for a reply Parkerson said that Mary Barnaby had drowned herself, adding that she had been married to Richard's brother. Matters supposedly secret within the family were not so secret in a wider sphere. Richard Randalsome went in search of his brother.

John Randalsome had recently left the residential employ of Parkerson and now maintained a farm at Bungay while living with his parents at Broome; his sister, brother-in-law and niece – the Minns family – lived next door. Tall, gaunt and balding, he was forty years of age and, like most in the area, had worked in husbandry all his life. Recently he had been the talk of the neighbourhood as rumours spread of his secret marriage to Mary Barnaby, rumours that had reached his girlfriend, 35-year-old Elizabeth Punchard, a maidservant in the employ of Mr Margitson at Ditchingham. He had reassured her that the stories were false. He would soon have to speak to others on the subject.

Richard Randalsome would say that he found his brother with two horses on the Bungay road and demanded to know if he was married to Mary Barnaby.

John said, 'Yes.'

Richard said, 'My master says Mary has drowned herself.'

John supposedly replied, with tears in his eyes, 'Dear me, you do not say so.'

More than a month later Richard, by then in dire trouble, admitted that his brother's first response to news of his wife's death had been, 'I know it'.

The brothers spoke again at their parents' home in the company of both parents and the Minns family, clearly a conference in anticipation of future interviews.

A Mary Barnaby's Bed-chamber.
B The Parlour Window where she was last seen sewing, and where the candle was found after the Murder.

C The Wash-house where the poisoned kettle was placed.
D The Path leading to the Pond

E The Wash-house door that was left open.

The Barnabys' farmhouse, sketched and annotated.

The pond, sketched and annotated.

F The Pond, which is at the back of the House.
G The Path leading from the Pond to the House.

H The Gap in the Fence through which Randalsome used to come when visiting Mary Barnaby by night.

Richard went back to work in his field for an hour before, consumed with curiosity, setting off for Thwaite, on the way finding his brother riding up behind him. John passed without speaking but then stopped his horse, waiting for his brother, who was on foot, to catch up. John asked Richard to look after his money and gave him two sovereigns, two half-crowns and a sixpence. He gave no explanation but rode off. One explanation is he expected to be arrested.

At the Barnaby farmhouse Richard found his brother crying in the kitchen. They went outside and John asked Richard to inform Elizabeth Punchard of the death but not to tell her that he had been married to Mary. Richard refused. John said that he had arranged to meet Mary that night but had told her not to stay up if he was not there by ten o'clock, and, he said, he had not gone there.

Charles Garneys conducted a post-mortem that revealed Mary was six to seven months pregnant. He found a jagged wound to the left temple – cutting through to the bone, a considerable contusion below and behind the left ear, a wound over the right eyelid, which was swollen, and a wound on the upper lip with a contused gum. There were marks on her right arm and neck, and her gown had been torn at the shoulder. He concluded the wounds were not sufficient to cause death. She had been thrown unconscious into the pond and had drowned. He opined that the temple wound had come from the blunt end of a hard instrument, such as the stake used to retrieve the body, which had the appearance of being bloodstained. In 1840 that was as far as forensic evidence went.

Constable James Earl of the new Rural Force (now the Norfolk Constabulary) arrived at ten o'clock on the Friday morning and saw the body and John Randalsome. He walked with Randalsome to the nearby field and back to the stack-yard, a contrived or fortuitous arrangement we do not know, but the constable went back to the field to study the footprints left by Randalsome. They matched those noted by Stowards and Hindle. He went back to Randalsome and removed his boot, taking it to the field, where it fitted exactly into the print staked by Stowards. And Earl knew his boots. He had been a shoemaker for ten years before joining the new police.

Constable Earl next went to the pond in the company of John Randalsome and John Barnaby and while there, Randalsome asked, 'Where are the stakes?'

The constable said, 'Stakes! I don't see any stakes.'

John Barnaby said, 'We have taken care of one.'

Randalsome made no further comment.

Constable Earl suspected John Randalsome from the outset; he had stopped him on the road from Thwaite to Broome between two and three o' clock on the morning of Monday, 15 June, when Randalsome admitted he had been visiting Mary. The constable reported his suspicions to Superintendent Henry Hubbersty at Loddon.

John Randalsome made another attempt to get a message to Elizabeth Punchard. At noon he saw his 45-year-old sister, Mary Minns, at her next-door cottage and said,

> I wish you would go up to that girl Punchard and tell her if any-one went up to her, to say I had nothing to do with her except as a fellow servant, and if anyone asked whether I had had any money off her to say at different times when we lived at Mr Parkerson's.

Mary Minns left on her errand. She forgot half the message and had to go back the next day to speak about the borrowed money.

That Friday evening Richard Randalsome told the Minns family, 'She is murdered from what people say, and I am afraid it will be laid on my brother.' He, and they, obviously said much more; this is just an admitted snippet. Richard Randalsome would also admit that, on this same evening, in his parents' home, John asked him if the police had said anything about poisoning. Richard told him the subject had not been mentioned, which caused John to say that he knew more about 'that' [arsenic in the tea-kettle] than anybody.

His mother warned, 'John, you have got some poison in your box and the house may be searched.'

John replied, 'That is gone.' It follows that James Barnaby was truly innocent of attempting to poison his daughter. Her husband had placed the arsenic in the tea-kettle on a late-night visit.

At nine o'clock that evening John called at Richard's home at Broome and took back his money. Undoubtedly there occurred another confer-ence concerning the future – what was to be said, and by whom, and how much did the police know?

At ten o'clock that Friday evening Superintendent Hubbersty went to the Barnaby cottage and asked to see the body. His uniform and rank did not impress a certain Maria Fisher, who can only have been the new housekeeper, and she refused him access, quoting surgeon Garneys as her authority.

The rebuffed superintendent returned at half past ten the following morning and saw the body. He ordered the pond to be emptied. His next objective was John Randalsome, everybody's suspect.

The suspect rode up to his brother's house in a gig that Saturday morning and declared his intention to hire Mr Drake, a solicitor. He said, 'These people want to lay this job on me. What a fool you must be to say anything about me giving you that there money.' Richard protest-ed, or so he said, that he had not said anything and John retorted that Mrs Gower (Mary's sister) had 'mobbed' him over the money. John then said, according to Richard, 'If you are called before the jury and asked anything about the money, say I lent you five shillings.'

Charlotte Gower had indeed upbraided John Randalsome over her sister's death. She had known of the secret marriage, told as a sister's confidence, and when John defensively said, 'They are going to lay this job on me' she had venomously replied, 'They are going to lay on right!'

John Randalsome was still determined to get a message to Elizabeth Punchard. At eleven o'clock he turned up at the Ditchingham home of her mother, asking her to tell her daughter 'to say she had no acquaintance with me only as a fellow servant'. He said it 'would hurt me very much' if she said otherwise and he was innocent of drowning Mary Barnaby.

Mrs Punchard said, 'You have got my daughter's money.'

Randalsome promised that her daughter would 'have it again'.

At half past three that afternoon, Superintendent Hubbersty, in the company of Constable Earl, saw John Randalsome on the road near James Barnaby's farmhouse.

Before Hubbersty could speak Randalsome blurted out, 'God strike me dead; I am innocent of this job.'

The superintendent replied, 'No one makes a charge against you.' He then asked where Randalsome was on Thursday night and Randalsome described drinking in a public house at Bungay, checking his horse in its field, going to a beer shop at Duke's Bridge, checking horses in another field and leaving there at eleven o'clock to go home via Wainford Mills. He said his mother and his niece saw him arrive home at half past eleven.

Superintendent Hubbersty didn't believe him, obviously. He arrested him. It meant John Randalsome would appear at the inquest as a prisoner, a pointer for the jury and probably what Hubbersty intended.

Constable Earl removed Randalsome's boots, prompting Randalsome to question why he wanted them.

'To show the coroner,' replied Earl.

'I will warrant these boots were never in that field, only when you were with me,' said Randalsome.

The inquest took place at the *Swan Inn* at Loddon under Coroner John Muskett, beginning on Sunday 21 June. Circumstantial evidence pointed to John Randalsome as the killer of his wife, nullified by his alibi. His father, also named John, claimed to be a sound sleeper and did not know, he said, what time his son came home on the night of the murder but his mother, Elizabeth Randalsome, elderly and frail, said her son arrived home at half past eleven. His nineteen-year-old niece, Harriet Minns, living next door, said she had been sitting up sewing a bonnet and saw her uncle come up the path at half past eleven.

On this Sunday John Randalsome was in transit in a carriage escorted by constables Samuel Howard and James Earl. On the road they saw Richard Randalsome, and John called out to his brother, 'This girl Punchard is bringing me to all this'. They continued and within a short time saw Randalsome's brother-in-law, James Minns. This time John

Randalsome called out, 'This girl Punchard will hang me if she can.' They continued and Randalsome said to Constable Howard, 'God strike me dead but I'm innocent of this here job.'

Richard Randalsome saw Elizabeth Punchard on that Sunday, though he would be in chains in Norwich Castle before he admitted it. He claimed she sent for him, which she denied. They discussed the evidence she should give at the inquest and Richard asked her if she had given his brother money and she agreed she had, asking his advice about how much she should admit to when questioned. He told her to say it was only £2 (it was £14).

John Randalsome said little at the inquest, shielded by his right not to incriminate himself, but he was not averse to some injudicious remarks away from the formal proceedings. On the Monday he observed to Superintendent Hubbersty that his wife had a savings account and he was damned if he would not have it (£55 had already been withdrawn). On the Tuesday he told the superintendent, 'If I get out of this job I will be married again directly and shall not go into mourning nor put a piece of crape around my hat for her, and I shall come down with a horse and cart and fetch away all her things.' On the way to Norwich Castle he said to Hubbersty 'I dare say you will tell the magistrates but I don't care; if I get out of this job I will be married to the girl Punchard – you may tell her so.' This freedom of speech by the suspect went further. He changed his story of his route home on the fatal night, telling Hubbersty that he had not gone via Wainford Mills but by Falcon Meadows and Ditchingham Dam. Hubbersty measured this new route and found it to be just over a half-mile further than the first one offered by Randalsome. And it led straight to Thwaite. Why did he suddenly admit to a route that took him to the murder? Had he realised that witnesses to his real route were forthcoming?

At twelve midnight on the Tuesday the jury recorded a verdict of murder by person or persons unknown and John Randalsome anticipated freedom. It never came. Superintendent Hubbersty obtained a warrant to return him to Norwich Castle.

As Randalsome left the public house he stepped back from his police escort and spoke hurriedly to the landlord, John Fisher. He said, 'I wish you would see the girl Punchard and tell her not to say anything against me; don't say I sent you as I am afraid she will hang me.'

Fisher asked if Punchard 'knew enough'.

Randalsome replied, 'I am innocent of this, but if you will do it I will make you a handsome present when I return.'

Five magistrates were convened to examine the case and hearings took place throughout July, again using the *Swan Inn*. A publicised reward of £100 and a free pardon for any accomplice giving evidence suggests the magistrates were not overly confident. They were not impressed with Richard Randalsome's evidence and committed him to

Norwich Castle as an accessory to murder. They also took a poor view of the evidence of Mary Minns and Elizabeth Punchard and sent them to the Wymondham Bridewell, Punchard leaving in floods of tears.

Richard Randalsome returned to the hearing, in chains alongside his brother, suitably chastened and admitting his conspiracy with Elizabeth Punchard. There is a strong suspicion that at this point he broke ranks and unofficially told of the falsity of his brother's alibi.

Harriet Minns certainly broke the alibi, and in doing so pointed the finger at her uncle. Under cross-examination she said that 'no one would draw her [Mary] to the dyke [pond] but them that knew her', and accordingly Harriet now thought she had been confused over different Thursday nights and it was the previous week she saw her uncle arrive home at half past eleven. She made a deposition accordingly.

Elizabeth Randalsome, mother of John and Richard, still said that John came home at half past eleven but there is no deposition in her name. Her evidence had become untenable.

Richard Randalsome made depositions on 13 July and 29 July, and even then it is doubtful he told the complete truth of what he knew and did.

Mary Minns, brought back from Wymondham Bridewell, stubbornly refused to go beyond 'Yes' or 'No' when answering questions, a session described as a 'tedious cross-examination'. Her deposition, made on 13 July, took the case no further than a grudging admission of taking her brother's message to Punchard.

A tearful Elizabeth Punchard said that John Randalsome had promised to marry her five years ago when they were in the employ of Mr Parkerson. She agreed he had borrowed several sums of money from her amounting to £14. After the poisoning case she heard rumours he was married to Mary Barnaby and taxed him about it. He denied the rumours and said the poisoning was a disgrace to the Barnaby family. He had, however, admitted that he had 'a young one coming' and when she asked if the mother was Mary Barnaby he refused to say. She said that in January she went with Randalsome to *The Dove* public house at Poringland near Norwich and, at his instigation, passed herself off as Mrs Randalsome. She was cross-examined by magistrates on an arrangement to travel to Norwich with John Randalsome on 27 June, denying that the purpose of the trip was for them to be married.

John Randalsome contributed little to the proceedings and was, of course, not obliged to. When asked if he had any questions following the evidence of surgeon Garneys he replied, 'No, I have nothing to say; I was not there; I know nothing about it; I wish I did.' In reply to his brother's evidence he said, 'No, my brother has said that which is false.'

Witnesses gave an insight into Randalsome's movements and temperament on the Thursday evening, starting in *The Swan* public house at Bungay. Emily Page said she spoke to him because he looked troubled,

The publicised reward, and a pardon for accomplices.

WILFUL MURDER.

£100 Reward

AND

HER MAJESTY'S FREE PARDON

WHEREAS early in the morning of Friday, the 19th day of June, 1840, some Person or Persons wilfully and maliciously Murdered MARY the Wife of JOHN RANDLESOME, by violent blows and casting her into a pond on the premise of her Father, James Barnaby, situate in the parish of Thwaite, in the county of Norfolk, between Loddon and Bungay.

A Reward of £100 will be paid by Her Majesty's Government to any person who shall give such Information and Evidence as shall lead to the discovery and conviction of the Person or Persons guilty of the said Murder.

Her Majesty's free pardon will be granted to any accomplice (not being the person who actually committed the Murder) who shall give such evidence as shall lead to the conviction of the principal Offender or Offenders.

By Order of the Magistrates of Loddon and Clavering district.

JAMES COPEMAN, their Clerk

Loddon, 2nd July, 1840.   (2974

but when she mentioned the poisoning attempt against his wife he denied Mary Barnaby was his wife, saying, 'She is not my wife – never will be. I will be damned if she is or ever will be.' He told her he did not care anything about 'old Barnaby or his daughter'.

James Smith said that he and Randalsome were drinking together and were 'both a little the worse for liquor' when a Mr Brock from Ditchingham came in and said to Randalsome, 'You are a married man, you know you are'. A fight was only averted by Brock leaving the establishment, following which Smith turned to Randalsome and said, 'You mean to say you are not married?'

Randalsome replied, 'No, I am not married at this present time, that I may be I cannot say.'

Page witnessed the altercation with Brock and again spoke to Randalsome about his rumoured marriage.

Randalsome said, 'If anything happen I shall get married in three weeks' time to the Margitson servant [Punchard].' He said it would be 'Saturday fortnight' (27 June). He asked Page to be a bridesmaid but she deemed him 'agitated by liquor' and refused.

Randalsome left *The Swan* at twenty past nine and turned up at the Duke's Bridge beer shop of George Brighton just before ten o'clock. He stayed about half an hour without drinking anything. He sat on a long stool with his head down and his hat pulled down over his eyes. Brighton quite naturally spoke to a man who showed no sign of being a paying customer.

Randalsome said, 'I never had a harder job in my life to keep my hands off anyone than I have had tonight; a man has been accusing me of being a married man and carrying on an acquaintance with another woman.' He left without further explanation, or buying anything.

At a quarter past ten Randalsome met Ann Fitzgerald and Mary Copsey, whom he knew, on the road to Falcon Meadows. He invited them to take a drink with him at a nearby public house but they declined.

John Randalsome in the dock.

At a quarter past eleven he met Samuel Fairhead on a footpath at Falcon Meadows and, knowing each other, they each said 'Goodnight'.

Another witness did not see Randalsome that night but was possibly close to him. Samuel Simmons lived in his master's house at Thwaite, alongside a rarely used, gated footpath that ran alongside fields to the Barnaby farmhouse. At half past twelve the gate squeaked and his master's dog barked. Simmons looked out of the window but in the darkness could not see anybody.

Randalsome's attitude throughout the proceedings had been one of confidence, frequently talking with Mr Drake, his solicitor, afterwards apparently unmoved by his trips with Superintendent Hubbersty through a yelling crowd to the castle. And he had not given up trying to condition Elizabeth Punchard's evidence. At Norwich Castle he tried to recruit a fellow prisoner to take a message to Elizabeth. His efforts came to the notice of the turnkeys and a trap was set.

On 9 July turnkey James Goodchild placed himself in the cell above Randalsome's in the company of two prisoners, Philip Goddard and John Lord. Goddard was due for release and the target for Randalsome's entreaties, which he called unseeingly through the bars of his cell. Goddard could not write but Lord could and, armed with pen and paper supplied by the prison governor, and corroborated by Goodchild, he wrote down all that Randalsome said, some of which is noted here.

> Go to the young woman and tell her to say that I never promised her marriage ... and tell her to come to me as soon as I am set at liberty ... tell her if she do say I promised her marriage that will be sure to hang me ... tell her what she have said is what have kept me in prison.

This rare picture shows the prison inside Norwich Castle, closed in 1887 and later demolished to house the Castle Museum. Randalsome spoke through the bars of his cell to the occupant above him. Norfolk Museums & Archaeology Services

The next day he continued to plead and the listeners continued to record. He said, 'I want you to tell her that I thought it very hard when I see her with the constables that she would not turn to look at me … there is no one but she can do me any hurt, therefore she had better tell a lie than I should be hanged, and tell her if I get clear to bring a few shillings with her so that we may go home comfortable together.' He promised Goddard £2, then £5.

At the end of the witness examinations the magistrates committed Randalsome to the Summer Assizes at Norwich, a decision he accepted calmly, and he was driven away through a noisy crowd.

The trial of John Randalsome took place at the Norwich Shirehall in the first week of August, previewed by Mr Justice Patteson and a Grand Jury under the foremanship of Lord John Townshend. (Grand juries were abandoned in 1913.) Mr Justice Patteson said he found the Randalsome case 'mainly resting on circumstantial evidence, which had to be carefully sifted'. The Grand Jury duly found a true bill.

John Randalsome appeared strangely confident at his trial and it is pos- sible he thought his alibi would be restored. He complained bitterly when neither his mother nor niece gave evidence. Mr Evans led for the prosecution, with a smoother task than Mr Prendergast, who led for the defence.

Superintendent Hubbersty admitted under cross-examination that he had not at any time cautioned Randalsome. He said that the prisoner had always spoken voluntarily and he had merely listened, an explanation in line with judicial disapproval of police questioning prisoners.

Richard Randalsome had rebounded between deciding what should be admitted, what should be denied and what should be invented. The hearsay rule saved him from some embarrassment, though perhaps not family wrath, especially if he 'threw down' the alibi as the press speculated. He survived without a more damaging cross-examination, probably because he could be seen as unreliable, and in the end – inconsequential.

Elizabeth Punchard similarly survived without further evasion or distress, only too aware of the perils of conspiracy and perjury.

Mr Prendergast made a strong speech lasting one hour and forty minutes in which he said that his client saying 'Goodnight' to witness Fairhead was hardly the act of a man planning murder and that Randalsome had never shown ill feeling to his wife and there was 'no proof of him being of a cruel and malicious disposition'. He said no reliance should be placed on the footmarks in the field and Mary Barnaby might have been murdered by an outsider. He finished by claiming that only suspicion existed against his client and asked the jury to consider whether there really was 'clear and unquestionable evidence of guilt'. He called several witnesses to his client's good character.

Mr Justice Patteson summed up and asked the jury to consider 'that if a stranger had done this what could be his object?'

The jury took fifteen minutes to return a verdict of 'Guilty'.

In time-honoured form Randalsome was asked if he had anything to say before sentence was passed and he replied, 'I was not near the premises by more than three mile; and I never saw my wife from twelve o'clock on the Wednesday night to twelve o'clock on the Friday morning when she was dead. That is all I can say.'

Mr Justice Patteson said that he entirely concurred with the jury's verdict. He told Randalsome, 'It was your duty to have owned her to the world.' He sentenced him to death by hanging and said he would not flatter him that the sentence would not be carried into effect. The *Norfolk Chronicle* noted that the prisoner received the sentence with 'imperturbable firmness'.

There exists in the National Archives a letter from the chief constable, Colonel Oakes, dated 9 August, 1840, to 'Phillipps'. The Home Secretary of the day was Constantine Henry Phipps. Colonel Oakes wrote: 'I take the liberty of asking whether under the circumstances, by which such information and conviction were obtained, the reward in question will be given, if so, to beg for your instructions in reference to it.' The case papers accompanied the letter. A scribbled note on the chief constable's letter says, 'Nothing to be done on this.' So somebody had claimed or enquired about the reward, and didn't get it. Who? Harriet Minns did abandon her alibi evidence after the reward was offered. And Elizabeth Punchard, although devious and averse to the complete truth, did not, after all, lie on John Randalsome's behalf, despite his communication efforts. And his brother in the end did him no favours and may have ruined a fabricated alibi. And William Stowards knew that Mary expected Randalsome on the fateful night because she had told him, an early pointer if not admissible evidence. We shall never know.

John Randalsome's time in Norwich Castle awaiting execution, set for 22 August, excited the interest of those seeking confession and redemption of his soul, including the *Norfolk Chronicle*, this worthy newspaper going so far as to send a reporter as an observer to his waiting time, or deputising an observer as a reporter, the result being the same. Reports that Randalsome briefly went on hunger strike were not confirmed by the newspaper but they did note that he 'displayed none of the fervour of vital religion, or the deep humility of true repentance' and 'exhibited a sad levity of conversation and conduct to those who had the care of his safe custody'.

On 17 August his parents, sister and niece visited him to make their farewells, yet he remained confident of a reprieve. He gave them a handkerchief and asked that it be passed to Elizabeth Punchard with a request that she visit him. She didn't.

Some accounts note a petition to the Home Secretary, possibly confused with his lawyers presenting an appeal for clemency, which the Home Secretary referred to Mr Justice Patteson. True to his word, the judge refused to commute the sentence he had passed.

The Reverend James Brown, chaplain at Norwich Castle, persistently and unsuccessfully sought to achieve Randalsome's reconciliation with the Christian faith, to which a confession would be helpful. The *Norfolk Chronicle* referred to Randalsome's defiance as 'unsatisfactory and obdurate', adding, 'A more ungenerous and thoroughly selfish disposition could not be portrayed.'

Randalsome blamed his brother for convicting him 'by perjury' and reviled others for his predicament, including his previous master, Carter Parkerson. He spitefully admitted that he had assisted men to steal goods from Parkerson. Informed on the Wednesday that his appeal had failed, he refused to accept the decision and insisted that the chaplain and the coroner write to the Home Secretary.

On Saturday, 22 August 1840, John Randalsome knew that he had run his time. Last appeals for him to confess and accept religion came to nought and the *Norfolk Chronicle* said he was 'destitute of every right principle of honesty or religion, and totally unworthy of credit in his last moments.' Yet he did give a glimpse of recognition of guilt, if not an acceptable confession. He promised that he 'would not die with a lie on his tongue.' He didn't. He made no more denials. He said nothing.

Minutes before twelve noon John Randalsome walked in a procession of officials with the Reverend Brown leading and chanting from the Prayer Book, entering the castle yard and turning to the turnkeys' side room for pinioning, then through the main gates, moving 'slowly with a feebleness of step', climbing the steps to the gallows before a restless crowd estimated at 6000. He looked from side to side, his face haggard, tears in his eyes, lips tightly closed, the expression disappearing under white cloth. The trapdoor opened and John Randalsome plunged to his death and, in his distorted mind, without a lie on his lips.

Such cases of denial often in later years create speculation concerning guilt or innocence. Not in this case. John Randalsome had been seen as a scheming, rapacious man without scruples, a manipulator of women and a liar and cheat. His jury had been the people of his Norfolk countryside.

Today the Barnaby farmhouse remains as a monument to a rural tragedy, reputedly visited by the apparition of a woman through a wall at the point where the old wash-house door had been left open. Successive owners and workmen speak of an uneasy feeling of being watched and never alone in the building. To some the unloved and misused Mary Barnaby (Randalsome) still has a presence.

Norwich Castle towers over cattle pens and a lone figure. From the main doors to the bridge was a short walk, for some their last. Norfolk Museums & Archaeology Services

CHAPTER 6

The New Police

The Murder of a Yarmouth Shopkeeper, 1844

In the late hours of a cold November night in 1844 policemen explored the streets and rows of Great Yarmouth by the pale light of their oil lamps, unsuspecting that routine was about to transcend into horror. Dressed in leather top hats and long coats, carrying a wooden stave, they were part of a force nearly nine years old, representing an order not entirely accepted by the people. On this night they would be crucial to the truth of a savage murder and, as the philosopher Voltaire observed, 'the dead are owed the truth'.

A few minutes after eleven o'clock Constable Samuel Waller spoke to John Sayer in the Market Place, a civil and brief exchange only. Waller moved on and Sayer saw three young men walking quickly towards the rows leading to Howard Street. He knew them as Robert Royal, James 'Jigger' Hall and James Mapes, all of nefarious reputation, particularly Royal. They disappeared into Black Swan Row.

Around half past midnight, Constable George Layton saw Samuel Yarham, a local shoemaker, walking from the direction of the Market Place to the beachside of the town. Who else Layton saw, and how well, would never be satisfactorily resolved, an issue to be examined later.

Some ten minutes after Layton's observation, George Knights, a watchman at a tanning yard, saw two men walking from the direction of the Market Place towards the beach, one much taller than the other, the shorter carrying something. Knights saw another man walking behind them and the day would come when he would believe that man to be Samuel Yarham. Knights watched the first two going onto the beach and stooping, but then turned away to investigate a noise on the property he was guarding. (A barrister would conclude that Yarham made that noise to distract Knights.) When Knights looked again at the beach the men had gone. He thought the tall man looked like Robert Royal and the other might have been James Mapes. Constable Layton was now in *The Feathers Tap* public house drinking a half-pint of porter, where he saw 'Jigger' Hall lying on a bench apparently unwell.

At one-thirty in the morning Constable Waller saw Robert Royal in Charlotte Street (now Howard Street North, site of the current police station), walking from the direction of Market Row. Waller was not to

Yarmouth rows in the nineteenth century were narrow, squalid and well populated.
Norfolk County Council Library & Information Services

know that he had disturbed a signal between Royal and a head poking from a window, a head that was quickly withdrawn upon sighting the policeman. At around this time Constable Layton saw Hall walking into the Market Place in the company of Jeremiah 'Gipsy' Cooper and another man and a woman. Hall brazenly wished the constable 'Good morning'.

Waller met up with Constable William Johnson and they walked along Howard Street to Harriet Candler's grocery shop near the junction with Market Row. Johnson tried the shop shutters, the first time he had tested the security of the premises that night despite passing five times since eleven o'clock. Now, at two o'clock, Waller noticed that the folding door of the shop had not folded shut. Sacking pinned over the fanlight had dropped into the door aperture. Waller pushed the door open. Two policemen peered into a dark, silent interior.

Johnson lit a candle and they began manoeuvring around the tiny shop, calling softly, then more loudly, tapping staves on the counter, working their way to the back room, tapping staves on the partition to the sleeping quarters, all for nothing. Just a brooding silence! They saw that the bed had not been slept in, though a depression indicated that somebody had recently sat upon it. Johnson left to look in the outside yard, returning perplexed, standing by the counter and becoming aware of something sticky under his feet. He peered over the counter.

Harriet Candler, a 43-year-old widow, sat hunched behind her counter, covered in blood, her head smashed and her throat sliced open. An empty till drawer stood against a sack of flour and a bloodstained towel lay over a cask, as if somebody had wiped their hands. Never was a scene so obviously one of murder. The Great Yarmouth Borough Police, inexperienced, untrained and subservient to investigating magistrates (similarly untrained and inexperienced), were about to embark on an investigation that would reveal the simplicity and inadequacy of nineteenth-century procedures, and the failings of those who had to apply them. Resolution of whose hand had done Harriet to death would not come until 1846.

Although Harriet ran her shop single-handed she shared the building. William Catchpole, an attorney-at-law, lived on an upper floor and his housekeeper, Sarah Yarham, and her husband Samuel, had rooms next to and below him. Whilst Catchpole was sufficiently removed to be undisturbed by two policemen calling and knocking their staves, the Yarhams were more proximate. It would be a surprise to learn that they had had not been out and had not heard anything.

Constable Johnson ran to the police station at the Town Hall and Sergeant John Willamant accompanied him back to Howard Street. A close inspection of the body revealed a length of line over the arms and a bloodstained knife nearby. The line would never be satisfactorily explained but conclusions may be drawn. The knife would be identified as the lard knife from the shop. Willamant sent for his chief officer – Superintendent Benjamin Love, surgeon Harry Worship, and the mayor and deputy coroner.

Worship found that Harriet's skull had been fractured by blows to the back and front and two cuts of 'considerable violence' had severed the throat. The forefinger of one of Harriet's hands had been sliced off, presumably a defence wound. At two-thirty in the morning the surgeon thought she had been dead three to four hours. He thought the blunt and sharp ends of a hammer may have caused the head injuries.

Sergeant Willamant provoked an appearance from Samuel Yarham by persistently ringing the shop bell, until Yarham poked his head out of an upper window. Told that something serious had happened Yarham went to the top floor to inform William Catchpole, and they both came down to the now-crowded shop.

William Catchpole said that he had dined out that evening and on his return at about half past one Yarham had let him in. Yarham said he had stayed awake waiting for Catchpole and tending his wife, who had been ill. He said he had gone into the shop at a quarter past ten and bought two rush lights from Mrs Candler. He had not seen or heard anything

79 Howard Street awaiting demolition in 1971. Colin Tooke

unusual and Catchpole's dog had remained undisturbed, despite its reputation as a 'furious' animal.

Catchpole said that on the previous night his dog had barked and had been quietened by Yarham and the next morning Harriet Candler had said she heard footsteps in the yard. The now-strangely subdued dog later became ill, thought by Catchpole to have been poisoned.

John Bales, Sergeant at Mace, added to the number of officials bustling around inside and outside the shop, and from the beginning he suspected Yarham of some involvement. During what the police called a 'strict search' of the premises Bales went into Yarham's rooms. He had in mind that a shoemaker should have a hammer with blunt and sharp ends. Magistrates would later criticise him for not finding one.

James Taylor, a pipemaker employed to remove the body, stepped on loose tobacco in unwrapped paper under the body, in time to prove evidential.

In the grey light of a new November day word of a brutal murder spread and a crowd gathered in Howard Street. As the day progressed the police searched 'vagrant houses and houses of ill-fame' and began tracing friends, acquaintances and customers of Harriet, quickly learning that she had just received a legacy of a cheque for £100 and £50 in

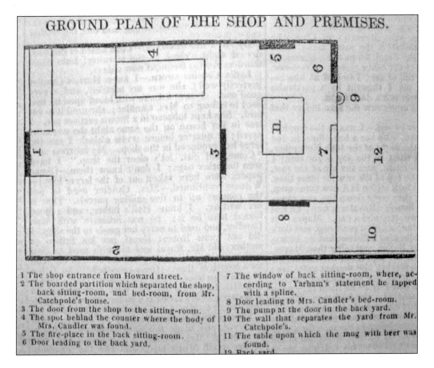

GROUND PLAN OF THE SHOP AND PREMISES.

1 The shop entrance from Howard street.
2 The boarded partition which separated the shop, back sitting-room, and bed-room, from Mr. Catchpole's house.
3 The door from the shop to the sitting-room.
4 The spot behind the counter where the body of Mrs. Candler was found.
5 The fire-place in the back sitting-room.
6 Door leading to the back yard.
7 The window of back sitting-room, where, according to Yarham's statement he tapped with a spline.
8 Door leading to Mrs. Candler's bed-room.
9 The pump at the door in the back yard.
10 The wall that separates the yard from Mr. Catchpole's.
11 The table upon which the mug with beer was found.
12 Back yard.

A plan of 79 Howard Street, drawn after the murder.

ten-pound notes (equivalent to nearly £8000 in 2006). But then her friend Margaret Edwards called to the shop after the murder, found a £100 cheque and five ten-pound notes in a bedroom drawer.

Beyond the murderer, or murderers, Harriet was last seen alive at 11 pm when she made her regular call to *The Black Swan*, obtaining her usual half-pint of porter. Sometimes she stayed a quarter or half an hour but on this night she said she was in a hurry and left with her porter, the drink to be found half-consumed in her back room. Seemingly she had disturbed her killer shortly after leaving the public house. She had died violently, horribly, but apparently quietly.

Busy as Monday, 18 November was, the next day was intensive and momentous. Upon Sarah Dick would hinge the whole investigation. She lived in the Town Battery opposite the beach with her soldier husband and fifteen-year-old daughter. While walking home with her daughter (also named Sarah) that morning she became less interested in the rolling surf of the North Sea and more in the sand hills. Two sets of footprints, one larger than the other, trailed some thirty yards over damp sand to a circle of disturbance. She curiously followed the prints and saw that somebody had been kneeling or sitting and, more importantly, burrowing. Fingermarks were visible. A broken earthenware pot and the bottoms of glass containers

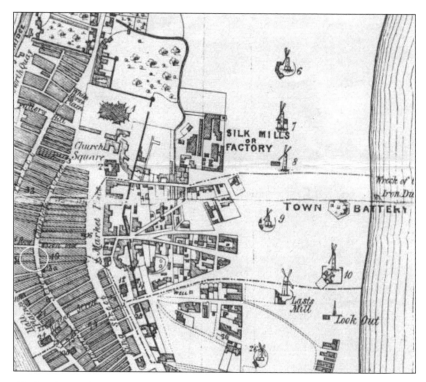

Fleeing from robbery and murder, 79 Howard Street, circled left, to the beach next to the Town Battery to hide the loot, right.

lay alongside. Markers? Something buried? Mrs Dick thought so.

As mother and daughter probed the sand they noticed a man watching them. He leaned on roadside palings, arms folded, legs crossed, unusually relaxed in what was a remote area far removed from the holiday seaside of the present day. And this was a cold, dull November day! Robert Royal watched intently.

Mrs Dick partially uncovered a canvas bag, which clinked as she moved it. She called out excitedly and her husband, John, and two other men came from the battery, followed by Royal. Her husband helped her pull the bag clear. It contained copper coins, a small purse and a card with the writing, 'Mrs Harriet Candler by rail'.

Royal said, 'There should be more yet' and began scrabbling in the sand, pulling out a smaller bag containing gold and silver coins. He said he would count the money but John Dick pushed his eager hand away, saying both bags should be taken straight to the police station.

Royal replied, 'There ought to be a cheque in there too', a knowledgeable comment that, wrong as it was, would take some explaining.

Royal proposed they take the money to John Dick's home but he was again overruled. Still in a possessive mood, he insisted that he carry the

[This Cut shews the spot where the money was found.]

Buried ill-gotten treasure; an 1845 picture.

bag he had found and so they set out for the police station, Mr and Mrs Dick and daughter, and Royal and a man reluctant to leave the excitement. They handed the sand-encrusted bags, the large one streaked with what looked like blood, to Sergeant Willamant. The large bag contained £2 17s 6d in copper. The other contained sovereigns, silver and copper coin amounting to £6 13s 10d.

Royal stayed in the police station. The police were not used to him voluntarily entering the place; and handing in stolen money! They arrested him and began rounding up his equally well-known associates. Before the day was out they had detained Jeremiah Cooper, James 'Jigger' Hall, James Hubbard and others, but not Mapes – yet! Police interviews were of necessity limited for these were times when magistrates interrogated prisoners.

There was more drama to come that day. In the afternoon Sarah Dick and her daughter again walked alongside the sand, stopping as they observed a man stooping over the place of their earlier discovery. He saw them and walked over, saying, 'It is very cold'. Mrs Dick agreed.

The man said, 'You are the woman that found the money.' Again Mrs Dick agreed.

The man said, 'All you have to do now is find the murderer.'

Mrs Dick replied, 'I wish to God I could.'

The man looked down and moved his foot back and forth, obviously torn with indecision, suddenly blurting out, 'I am the murderer'.

Mrs Dick scornfully replied, 'If you were you would not be so ready to tell me.' She asked his name.

He replied, 'You know me, don't you?'

She said she didn't know him and he slowly walked away, stopped, turned and rubbed his face, then turned and continued walking. Mrs Dick went immediately to the battery yard and spoke to fourteen-year-old William Seaman, a chimney sweep's boy. She pointed to the receding figure and asked the boy if he knew the man. Seaman looked, considered and said that it looked like Samuel Yarham.

A few days after the beach encounter Mrs Dick saw the mayor, William Palmer, and a magistrate, Caufue Davie, at the battery yard. She told them of the strange conversation and the perceived identity of Yarham. The mayor dismissively replied that it was just somebody 'tampering with justice'.

The inquest jury viewed the body and Harry Worship detailed the dreadful injuries to the head and neck. The bloodstained knife accounted for the neck but a hammer had not been found to match the head injuries. Worship said that although the head wounds were non-survivable she was still alive when her throat was cut, deduced because two pints of blood had flowed from the neck, indicating the heart was still beating.

The inquest jury returned a verdict of murder by person or persons unknown. Rumour in the town had Samuel Yarham as the murderer.

Samuel Yarham had been raised by 'poor parents' in Yarmouth and given a reasonable education up to the age of fourteen. He had lived near and been to school with Robert Royal. After learning the trade of shoe-maker he spent seven years in London, where he met his future wife, Sarah, who had been widowed. She was a political activist and Samuel assisted her in distributing socialist literature. Returning to Great Yarmouth with Sarah, he served one month in prison for stealing books. He and his wife obtained residential employment at Catchpole's house just two months before the murder.

On the Wednesday after the murder the magistrates discharged Royal, Hall, Cooper and Hubbard and ordered Yarham's arrest. Before the end of the week the police had rearrested Royal and Hall and detained James Mapes, who had not returned home on the night of the murder. Witnesses were coming forward or, more likely, being discovered. By the following Monday the press reported 'several persons in custody'. Many of these detentions would today live under the journalistic euphemism of assisting police with their inquiries.

The police took the footwear of Royal, Hall and Mapes and used them to make impressions in the sand, then asking Sarah Dick and her daughter to inspect them. Her view, never satisfactorily placed in evidence, indicated that Royal and Mapes had made the tracks. John Bales, convinced of Yarham's involvement, made impressions with Yarham's boots and claimed Mrs Dick had identified them. She hadn't. From George Knights's observations the third man, believed to be Yarham, didn't go onto the beach. Photographs and forensic examinations of the next century could have done wonders for this case.

John Critten, a turnkey at Yarmouth Gaol, reported that he had seen a spot of blood on the front of Royal's waistcoat and more blood spots on his sleeve. Nobody would be able to absolutely prove the spots were blood but it was accepted that people knew blood when they saw it.

George Todd, a milkman, visited Howard Street the morning after the murder and reported three drops of blood near the step of Harriet's back door. Again, it reflects upon the police's 'strict search', or had they already noted it? Further embarrassment came when William Catchpole, several days after the murder, found a spray of blood on the shop wall, 'as if a coat striking against it', and more on the kitchen door. The police had surely seen these marks but the press trumpeted Catchpole as a latter-day finder.

William Burgess had seen Royal looking in Harriet's shop window at about eight o'clock on the evening of the murder but magistrates passed over his evidence, to later incur a judge's wrath.

Christine Porrett said she had seen Royal 'a little after 9 pm' on the evening of the murder standing in Black Swan Row nearly opposite Harriet's shop. When he saw her he walked backwards into the row.

Two sightings precede Sarah Dick's discovery in the sand. At half past seven on the morning after the murder Frederick Barnby saw two men, in his words 'loitering near the Town Battery' and he asked the taller one the time. He believed that man to be Royal. Thomas Lewis, an innkeeper, knew Royal and Hall and at around eight o'clock that same morning he saw them walking from the direction of the beach.

Samuel Yarham, under official and public suspicion and in custody, was joined by his mother and two sisters helping or not helping with inquiries. Their examination by magistrates arose from the contents of the purse found in the larger bag. The bag indisputably belonged to Harriet Candler but ownership of the purse and a charm inside caused speculation. The charm had been wrapped in paper that bore a written scripture; the handwriting at first thought to be that of Yarham, which he denied, then thought by his sister Harriet to be that of their mother, which she denied. Sisters Mary and Harriet Yarham agreed that their brother always wrote a text from the scriptures when he wrote a letter, as did their mother.

Magistrates sensed a family conspiracy of some sort, especially as the sisters had met in Samuel's rooms on the evening of the murder. Mary said she left at 8 pm and Harriet said she left at a quarter to ten, after placing leeches on Sarah Yarham.

The magistrates released Yarham, an act thought by the *Norfolk Chronicle* to be 'a strange oversight', also his mother and sisters – if they had ever strictly been in custody. Samuel was soon rearrested, now followed into custody by his wife. William Catchpole dismissed them from his employ.

That Samuel Yarham was somehow concerned in the murder formed the thinking of public and magistrates. The mayor and Harry Worship went to Yarmouth Gaol to advise Yarham accordingly, requesting he tell the truth. There were several such trips by magistrates and they would be heavily criticised.

Pondering his position, Yarham decided that not hearing or seeing anything on the night of the murder would no longer be acceptable. He wrote to the mayor a succession of letters that in turn gained in description and detail on what he had seen and done that night. In his first letter he said that at ten minutes past eleven he had heard two or three persons moving about inside the shop, following which he had lit a candle and seen two men on the opposite side of the street, one of whom he recognised as Robert Royal. The other man, whom he did not know, he said, had a bundle under his arm. Yarham said the men walked away and were followed by another man and a woman. He explained that he had not said anything before because he knew 'what a desperate lot Royal was acquainted with'.

His second letter made the time twenty past eleven and in it he said he had heard a scuffle in the shop. He said he went round to the front door of the shop and saw a light inside but could not get in and when he knocked nobody answered. He went to the back yard and then back to the front door and saw Royal and a man he did not know leaving the shop. He claimed Royal said, 'Blast you, if you say anything I will serve you the same' and made off.

In a third letter Yarham said that Royal admitted taking money from the shop but did not know where 'the woman' was. In this letter Yarham thought the other man might be James Hall. Yarham did not admit that he went into the shop and found Harriet Candler dead: that came in a later admission.

Robert Royal, faced with Yarham's statements, said Yarham was a liar, as were the other witnesses who said they had seen him on the night in question.

James Hall defiantly said he was not guilty and James Mapes similarly declined to help with inquiries.

On 2 January 1845, Royal, Hall and Mapes, and Samuel and Sarah Yarham, were brought before magistrates with a view to committal for trial. The magistrates unusually, and without declared reason, ruled that proceedings should be in private, which upset the press and the crowd in the street outside. The *Norwich Mercury* reported that 'loud were the expressions of disapprobation at the exclusion of the public'. The

Mercury did, however, by some subterfuge, obtain an account of proceedings and it tallies with the depositions now in the National Archives.

Sarah Yarham was discharged without evidence being taken, presumably because there wasn't any against her. But there was enough to take the case forward in respect of the others. Samuel Yarham was charged 'on suspicion of being concerned with others in the wilful murder of one Harriet Candler', to which he replied with another version of what he saw and heard on that fateful night. He now said that when Royal came out of the shop he offered him a sovereign to keep his mouth shut and promised a share when 'we dole'. Yarham now referred to a third man with Royal and Hall and admitted finding Harriet Candler dead behind the counter.

Royal's solicitor called five witnesses to say that Royal was in *The Half Moon* public house on the evening of the murder and could not have been seen in various places as alleged by prosecution witnesses. He added that he could call many more witnesses to substantiate this alibi but did not wish to take up the court's time. Hall's solicitor called three witnesses to prove an alibi for his client and Mapes's solicitor called three alibi witnesses, one of whom was discounted when she forgot what she had said earlier. Public houses featured strongly in all the alibis.

Royal told the magistrates 'What Yarham has said is in every word false, likewise the other witnesses against me, particularly that of Sayer. I am perfectly innocent of the crime.' He turned on Yarham, snarling, 'You **** villain – it will come home to you yet.'

Hall said, 'All that I have got to say is I am not guilty.'

Mapes said, 'I do not say anything.'

Yarham said he would leave the case in the hands of his solicitor.

All four men were committed for trial and afterwards feelings ran against prosecution witnesses. John Sayer went to the Petty Sessions and appealed to magistrates for protection, saying Royal's father 'had collected indignant people' against him in the Market Place. Royal's father denied it. The Dick family were also harassed and abused and magistrates issued a warning, carried by the press, against any form of witness intimidation. It had little effect. Before the case had run its course several persons would be bound over or placed in custody for threats, particularly against the Dicks. Joseph Westgate and his wife (friends of Royal) were taken before magistrates for threatening the daughter with a knife, and John Dick detained two persons throwing stones at his house. The magistrates ordered policemen to visit the Town Battery every hour.

The contempt for Yarham went beyond the rabble-rousing cries of friends and relatives of his co-accused. Popular opinion still had him as the murderer, and the prospect of him 'getting off' was unpalatable.

The first test of the case against the four men came when Mr Justice Patteson reviewed the evidence before the Grand Jury at the Norwich Lent Assizes. He sourly commented that the evidence was not sufficient

A rogues' gallery. Top row: left, Samuel Yarham; right, James Mapes. Bottom row: left, James Hall; right, Robert Royal.

to make Yarham an accessory, and if the prosecution did not drop the charge and make him a witness there was no case against the others either. The Grand Jury accordingly discharged Yarham and the prosecution took him as a witness, infuriating all who believed in his guilt.

On Monday, 7 April 1845, Royal, aged twenty-four years, Hall, also twenty-four years, and Mapes, twenty-one years, stood in the dock in a packed courtroom and pleaded 'Not Guilty'. Royal and Hall were defended by Mr Prendergast and Mapes by Mr Crouch. The prosecuting barrister was supposed to be Mr Palmer, assisted by Mr O'Malley, but he turned up late in the day and was missing for most of the second day.

Before trying to prove that Royal, Hall and Mapes had committed murder the prosecution set about proving that Yarham had not. Mr O'Malley admitted that Samuel Yarham, aged thirty-four years, was a 'man of great moral depravity of character' but made the point that he 'could have possessed himself of her [Harriet Candler] wealth without even disturbing her in her sleep' and he had no need to engage in violent robbery. He said the murderers could have stepped over a low wall into Candler's yard and thence through an unfastened back door.

Yarham gave his evidence of seeing Royal and Hall leaving the shop but now added that he said to Royal, 'You have not killed her?' Royal allegedly replied, 'I hope not'. Yarham said he heard Royal call Hall 'Jigger'.

Mr Prendergast accused Yarham of being subversive and non-religious and of marrying a woman who had been the wife of a socialist. He made great play of Yarham's time in London and his wife's circulation of socialist literature, which led to a sharp exchange between him and Mr O'Malley. Mr Prendergast portrayed Yarham as a scheming liar who had provided contradictory accounts in instalments.

Other witnesses gave evidence with variations that irked the judge. He learned that magistrates had not been thorough in providing evidence through depositions and he severely castigated their methods. He threatened to fine them. Constable Waller made such an impression in the witness box Mr Justice Patteson told him that if he appeared before him again he would not believe anything he said on oath. One view could be that the prosecution was not doing very well, another that it was a shambles.

Mr Prendergast cleverly dealt with Royal's unguarded comment on the beach concerning the cheque, pointing out that if he had committed robbery and murder he would surely know the cheque was not in the bag, and the fact he knew it existed could have been known from general gossip surrounding the case. Mr Prendergast contemptuously announced that he had no need to call witnesses, inferring that the prosecution had no case or had made a hash of what they had got. Another sharp exchange took place between him and Mr O'Malley.

By now Mr O'Malley had had enough. He told the judge that in his view Hall was 'guiltless', to which the judge caustically replied that there was 'scarcely any case against Hall *and* Mapes'. The jury, however, said they would like to hear the whole case.

Proceedings were halted when several women fainted in the overflowing courtroom and a number of spectators were removed. At the end of the first day the jury were accommodated in the nearby *Bell Inn*.

The second day was no better for the prosecution. Mr Prendergast called six alibi witnesses for Royal, including Joseph Westgate, and another seven for Hall. Mr Crouch called seven alibi witnesses for Mapes. If these witnesses were to be believed the three accused were drinking in public houses on the night of the murder, and Maria Brown had prevented Mapes from going home by sleeping with him.

The judge in his summing-up pointedly referred to the accused men's haunts as 'places where robbers and murderers proceed'. He described the alibi witnesses with splendid understatement as 'not respectable' and found nothing good to say about Yarham. The jury's verdict was inevitable and had been for some time. They took all of three minutes to find all three men 'Not Guilty', the verdict greeted with applause from the public benches.

People spilled from the court into surrounding streets under the overshadowing Norwich Castle, chatting as they loitered. Royal, Hall and Mapes left in the cheering company of friends and relatives, possibly glancing at Castle Hill, where they could have met their end by virtue of Yarham's evidence. Amid this simmering excitement prosecution witnesses stole away anxious to avoid confrontations, but as George Knights walked over Castle Hill he met Yarham, who insisted on shaking his hand. At this point Knights became sure that Yarham was the third of the men he had seen approaching the beach.

Shaking Yarham's hand in the view of hundreds wishing to shake him by the neck understandably disconcerted Knights and he took refuge in a barber's shop in Orford Hill, followed by Yarham. A swelling, threatening crowd forced them from the barber's shop into a public house, where they were joined by Sarah Yarham. Her husband incautiously said that although Royal, Hall and Mapes had been cleared of murder they had not been cleared of robbery and that 'would linger and they would be sure to be found out'. The landlord then asked them to leave by the back way because the crowd outside were breaking his windows.

The Dick family were waiting to board a train at Norwich Thorpe Station when Mr and Mrs Yarham came over to them. Samuel wanted to shake hands with John Dick but was rebuffed, Dick saying he didn't know him.

Sarah Dick and her daughter now recognised Yarham as the man who had admitted the murder. She told her husband and he told her to hold her tongue, advising that she knew nothing and should have nothing to do with the man. Surprisingly, the Dick family had not viewed Yarham at the committal or trial. Even more surprising, the police had not arranged a viewing.

Having nothing to do with Yarham proved difficult when the Dick family found themselves in the same railway carriage as Mr and Mrs Yarham, especially when a solicitous Mr Yarham saw that Mrs Dick was lame and offered a stool to rest her foot. He spoke quietly, upsetting her by saying his solicitor was of the opinion that if they fetched him for the murder they would take her as well, believing she had hidden the money. Mrs Dick turned to her husband and he rounded on Yarham, telling him to leave them alone. The journey continued in an icy atmosphere. As they were leaving the carriage at Great Yarmouth Yarham told John Dick that if he saw anything in the newspapers about the Dicks he would come and tell them. An infuriated John Dick (he could read but his wife couldn't) said he didn't want to know and he didn't want Yarham coming anywhere near his family. The fact that Yarham later did so would solve the case.

The fall-out after the trial extended to the magistrates. Smarting over the judge's criticism, shaken by public opinion, they wrangled among themselves over the cost of the case, accusing and insulting each other but unitedly falling upon the police. Simon Cobb addressed his fellow magistrates thus: 'If due diligence had been used by the police of this town the murderer would have been discovered at an earlier stage.' Later a barrister would point out that if the magistrates had been more thorough in their examinations a better case would have gone to the Assizes, and if the mayor and Caufue Davie had taken Mrs Dick's identification (via the boy Seaman) seriously an earlier and better conclusion might have been reached.

Sergeant at Mace, John Bales, became a target for the magistrates' wrath. He had supplied a defending solicitor with maps and information (now standard practice) and the magistrates accused him of working for the defence, also of improper conduct concerning the unfound murder weapon, a more vaguely couched accusation. That a hammer was not the murder weapon was not appreciated at this time, when apportionment of blame was the priority.

Magistrates demanded that the conduct of Bales and constables Layton, Johnson and Waller be investigated, claiming that at the time of the murder Johnson and Waller were in 'that disgraceful house *The Globe*', and Layton was in *The Feathers Tap*. They pre-empted any investigation by voting for the dismissal of all four officers.

The borough council, duly prompted, suspended Bales for 'ill conduct', and appointed a committee to investigate his actions. He was reinstated after a finding that his conduct had been 'reprehensible' but had 'no improper motives'. Johnson remained in the force but Waller, doomed after the judge's comments, left to become a railway porter. Layton, dismissed for 'neglect of duty', became the landlord of *The King's Head* public house.

Yarham's recklessness now reached new heights. Still in April, he met Mrs Dick in the Market Place; an exceptional encounter because both of them had not ventured far in the face of public dislike – loathing in Yarham's case.

Yarham opened politely with, 'How do you do?'

Mrs Dick curtly said she didn't.

Yarham asked, 'Do any of these men, either Royal, Hall or Mapes, meddle with you?'

Mrs Dick replied not so much her as her daughter and asked if they had interfered with him.

Yarham replied, 'No, they know'd better.' He said he was going away because everybody blamed him and he was not so much to blame as the others.

Mrs Dick told him he was either the 'scoundrel himself' or he well knew who did it. She made to walk away, stopping as Yarham touched her on the shoulder and said, 'Stop, I'll tell you about it.' And he did, literally talking himself to death.

Yarham said that Royal, Hall and Mapes heard that Mrs Candler had got money and they wanted him to let them into her shop. They knew Catchpole was going to the *Angel Inn* in the Market Place and Mrs Candler regularly spent about half an hour in *The Black Swan*. They came to the back door at ten o'clock but the shop was still open and they backed off. Royal watched until Mrs Candler went into *The Black Swan*. Yarham then let them in and told them to go to the bedroom, where she kept her money.

Mrs Candler returned sooner than expected and Royal nipped out his candle and hid behind the counter. Hall and Mapes were searching the bedroom while Yarham sat on the bed. Mrs Candler went to the back room, put down her half-consumed beer and heard a noise from the shop. She saw Royal, said she knew him and asked what he wanted. He said he wanted half an ounce of tobacco and when she went to the tobacco jar he knocked her to the floor. Before she could recover, Hall rushed into the shop and struck her on the head with a pair of pincers. With the shopkeeper lying insensible Hall pinned sacking over the fanlights while the others searched (Yarham took some delight in telling Mrs Dick that the police had wasted their time searching for a hammer as the murder weapon).

Yarham said they got all the money they expected and left the woman for dead. Mapes went out first and joined a woman (Maria Brown?) in the street and he and Royal and Hall followed. They saw 'different people' they knew (more than came forward) and 'across the market Layton shone his light on them', (Layton didn't say that). Hall went to his father's house and Yarham, Royal and Mapes went to the beach to hide the money. Yarham said he turned back when he heard a noise.

Yarham told Mrs Dick that when he got home he heard Mrs Candler moaning and, fearing that 'she would surely know them all', he went into the shop, where she turned her eyes up to him (surely a pleading expression). He said he took the nearby lard knife and cut her throat, she losing a finger as she despairingly gripped the knife. He then went into his rooms and washed his hands.

Yarham said he waited for Royal to return and signal that the money was safely hidden and, putting his head out of the window, saw him approaching but also saw Constable Waller. He quickly withdrew his head.

A stunned Mrs Dick called Yarham a murderer and he replied, 'No, it was Hall and Royal beat her so with pincers'. He said Mapes only searched. He advised her to say nothing of his confession because his solicitor would see that she was 'fetched'. He said the authorities could not hurt him now because Royal, Hall, Mapes and himself had been cleared and, anyway, he had applied to the workhouse for money to leave town.

John Dick, told by his wife of the confession, ordered her to say nothing, saying, 'We have had trouble enough already'.

As Mrs Dick agonised over Yarham's confession he went, on 22 April, to the workhouse and received a grant of £3 to leave town. Taking himself to Gloucestershire, he must have thought a new life lay ahead.

Three months after Yarham's confession the burden of knowledge proved too great. Daughter Sarah Dick spoke to a magistrate and consequently Captain Love called upon her mother. Mrs Dick told all, which caused consternation among magistrates. Could Yarham now be tried? Would he invoke a defence of double jeopardy? He had been charged with murder and discharged by a Grand Jury, which wasn't the same as being found 'Not Guilty'. But he had admitted murdering a woman who had already been murdered inasmuch she was already dying when he cut her throat. By another view he was the original murderer because he was engaged in a common purpose with Royal and others. But they had been found 'Not Guilty'.

Magistrates were in a quandary and they eventually sought the opinion of the Attorney General. He wrote on 5 December 1845: 'Yarham is not entitled to protection from prosecution and should be apprehended and committed for trial. I cannot form any opinion as to the probability of the evidence securing a conviction.' He asked Mr Justice Patteson to forward his notes from the first trial to Mr Justice Maule, who would preside over Yarham's trial.

Yarham was arrested in Gloucestershire on 22 December and taken to Great Yarmouth for committal to the next Assizes, a year after his first appearance. He said he couldn't have met Mrs Dick in the Market Place because he couldn't walk the streets of Yarmouth without a mob being after him.

Yarham duly appeared before Mr Justice Maule at the Norwich Lent Assizes on Friday, 28 March 1846. Mr Dasent appeared for the defence and said he hadn't read the file because he had only been hired the previous evening and he therefore spoke with 'trepidation and alarm', which cannot have done much for Yarham's confidence.

Mr Palmer appeared for the prosecution and told the jury to 'dismiss all former circumstances from your mind', impossible in practice.

Mr Dasent mentioned reports of the case in London newspapers and 'all over the world' and attacked Yarmouth magistrates, saying they had kept back evidence and acted improperly and that they, not his client, should be on trial. He went on to accuse the mayor and magistrates of offering inducements and exerting pressure upon Yarham while he was in Yarmouth Gaol in December 1844. The magistrates' clerk, George Holt, suffered a severe cross-examination when it transpired that magistrates had visited Yarham in gaol as many as three times in one day with as many as six magistrates interviewing him at one time. Mr Dasent requested that Yarham's consequent letters to the mayor be disqualified as evidence. Mr Justice Maule said the magistrates had behaved irregularly and ruled the evidence inadmissible.

Mr Dasent next turned to Mrs Dick. He said she had fabricated the confession. She remained unshaken and repeated Yarham's words. There appeared no motive for her making up the confession and Mr Dasent was reduced to projecting scornful disbelief.

George Knights had got better as a witness. He now strongly believed that Yarham was the third man he saw heading towards the beach, though Mr Dasent referred back to earlier evidence when he had said he saw the man only as a shadow.

Ex-Constable Samuel Waller did not give evidence, which was not surprising after his previous castigation by Mr Justice Patteson. Ex-Constable Layton did give evidence and said he had told magistrates there were two other men with Yarham on the night of the murder but they did not put everything he said into his deposition.

In his concluding speech Mr Dasent said the magistrates 'had thrown overboard everything they had relied upon' and were now supporting 'a monstrosity of a case' and they had been 'strangely forgetful of their duty'.

Mr Justice Maule summed up by saying that the case turned on Mrs Dick. He said that Yarham's confession to her 'tallied exactly with what seemed to have been the case'.

The jury took five minutes to find Yarham 'Guilty'. A loud murmur in the court greeted the verdict followed by a loud 'hurrah' outside, causing a pale and trembling Yarham to turn his head.

Asked if he had anything to say, Yarham replied, 'I am innocent, so help me God'.

Mr Justice Maule addressed the ashen prisoner, 'You have, in conjunction with other persons, committed a deliberate and cruel murder ... I cannot find circumstances in the case to induce me to hold that any mitigation of the law can take place.' He solemnly advised, 'Your hours and minutes are numbered ... your attention to worldly causes must be in vain and useless.' He advised, as always, the prisoner to seek religious consolation and sentenced him to death by hanging. Yarham, now composed, left the courtroom calmly.

The *Norfolk Chronicle* hoped that the case would be a lesson to Yarmouth magistrates 'not to conduct examinations on a future occasion as they conducted Yarham's'.

In Norwich Castle awaiting execution Yarham wrote a series of letters, mainly to his wife but also to his father. He continued to protest his innocence, calling his identification by Mrs Dick and the boy Seaman 'an abominable lie'. He said he was at the inquest at the time and the police could have verified that if they had chosen to do so, and his barrister had failed to make this point. He wrote of Mrs Dick, 'My blood rests upon her head but I freely forgive her.'

Sarah Yarham visited her husband and was counselled by the castle governor not to mention the murder, which she promptly did. Acrimony followed as her husband complained he had been exhorted to confess by the prison chaplain, the Reverend James Brown. The chaplain protested that he had done nothing of the sort and Yarham admitted he had lied, saying he had expected to be pressured to confess. Yarham only ever made two confessions, briefly to Mrs Dick and her daughter near the Town Battery, if that truly was him, and in detail to Mrs Dick in Yarmouth Market Place when he presumed he was safe from prosecution. Many thought it incredible that he should die on the word of one woman, and advocated, and expected, a reprieve.

Yarham handed his wife a letter proposing she commit suicide with him, saying, 'We will die together ... I am determined not to hang.' She handed the letter to the governor and did not see her husband again. He sent her a farewell letter which concluded, 'Your affectionate but unhappy and innocent dying husband.'

At Norwich Castle on 11 April an enormous crowd, estimated at 30,000, waited for the last act in the saga. The execution was set for twelve noon and revellers from a nearby fair bolstered the waiting masses, people gaining vantage points in houses and trees and as far away as the tower of St Peter Mancroft. The new railway sold 1500 day-tickets from Great Yarmouth. A train from Wymondham brought 800 persons using bullock carts to make up the carriages.

Royal and Hall were spotted on Castle Hill and jostled by the crowd, so much so they fled into *The Golden Ball* public house, from which they were immediately ejected. Other places they went to also turned them out and the *Norwich Mercury* reported, 'The police were compelled to take the miserable beings in charge to secure their personal safety.'

Broadsheets abounded in the Yarham case. Norfolk Heritage Centre

Yarham emerged from the castle walking unsteadily in a procession headed by the Reverend Brown reading the funeral service. He was assisted to the gallows by the governor, George Pinson, and executioner William Calcraft. After a few minutes of prayer, adjusting the rope and feet, the trapdoor opened and he dropped, briefly struggled and then remained still.

After hanging for the customary hour Yarham was taken into the castle and buried in the grounds. Outside the walls an accumulating degree of disorder was described in *Norfolk Annals* as: 'Hundreds finished the day in riot and intoxication.'

The press called the scenes after the execution 'a scandalous character of proceedings' and a public meeting in St Andrew's Hall on 17 April, presided over by the mayor, voted to petition parliament for the abolition of capital punishment. A second motion sought to make executions a non-public event. No person present would see the first proposal come to fruition and it would be another twenty-one years before the second came to pass. People watching Yarham die would say they had seen justice done, perhaps forgetting about a thuggish gang leader and a man with pincers.

Governor George Pinson and turnkeys (warders) in Norwich Castle, a picture possibly taken when Pinson retired in January 1876. He had been appointed in December 1843 and supervised many executions, including that of Yarham. He died in 1879. Norfolk Museums & Archaeology Services

CHAPTER 7

The New Police

Death of a Soldier, 1880

Asoldier may envisage death as a consequence of his profession, invariably at the hands of an enemy on a battlefield in a foreign land. He could not foresee dying by the considered act of his fellow soldiers, in barracks, in his own country. The death of Private John Smith (as he called himself) of the 17th Regiment of Foot (Leicestershire) is a curiosity for other reasons: the *modus operandi* was unique, the apparent motives were, and still are, sensitive to conscience, religious beliefs and medical ethics, and, sensationally, the dead man gave evidence.

The crux of the case was Smith's illness, described as 'a loathsome disease', believed to have been contracted during his regiment's service in India, though nineteenth-century England was not without its own loathsome diseases, of which cholera, typhus and consumption (tuberculosis) were prime examples.

The 17th of Foot returned to England from India in 1879, to be

The cavalry barracks. Norfolk County Council Library & Information Services

billeted at the Cavalry Barracks (later renamed Nelson Barracks) in Norwich, situated in the appropriately named Barrack Street. The street today is much altered, the barracks long gone, but before its demise into a grassy plain of low-cost housing it was a bustling symbol of the power of the British Army, containing as many as 320 soldiers and 266 horses. For those who know where to look, part of the enclosing wall remains.

Private Smith, too ill to be moved, was left behind when his regiment moved from Norwich in the summer of 1880. A cavalry regiment, the 6th Inniskilling Dragoons, moved into the barracks and inherited the desperately ill infantryman. Two Dragoons, Private William Solly, aged twenty-three years, and Private Henry Pritchard, aged nineteen years, were assigned to hospital duties. They joined two soldiers of the Army Hospital Corps who already ministered to the sick in the barracks: Staff Sergeant William Alexander Browne, aged thirty-eight years, long serving with a good-conduct medal and scheduled for promotion, and Private William Davies, aged twenty-four years. The question is, did these four men seek to release a patient from an agonised and doomed life, perhaps remove the hindrance of his care, even realise a mercenary motive? Alternatively, they were victims of circumstances.

The drama of life and death was played out within two buildings inside the barracks in August 1880. The infirmary and the 'infectious ward' lay a measured thirty-four yards apart, the windows of the infirmary looking down eighteen feet into the ground-floor room where Smith lay in his bedridden state. A choice of windows offered infirmary patients different views into Smith's room.

The night of 3 August was warm and windows were left open in both buildings. Just before midnight a shrill cry of 'murder' carried from Smith's room. The majority of infirmary patients never left their beds that night, or did not admit so, either relying on the commentaries of others or remaining distinctly uncurious, but four soldiers were sufficiently roused to go to various windows and look into Smith's room. The gas lighting of that room had been turned down but three men could be seen around Smith's bed, one holding a sheet and another a pillow, while a fourth man stood at the head of the bed, recognised as Sergeant Browne by the watching Private Thomas Heap and Private William Logan. The other watchers, Private John Herriott and Private James Candy, could not identify any of the men, they said, though Candy did observe that three of them wore grey shirts and the fourth a white shirt. (Privates were issued with grey shirts. Sergeants had white shirts.) One of the men in Smith's room, believed to be Browne, closed the window and all four left, closing the door.

Private Solly appeared in the infirmary ward and ordered those lingering at windows back to bed, brusquely announcing there was 'nothing to see'. After he left, the sound of crockery breaking in Smith's room brought infirmary patients back to their windows, viewing greenish-blue flames flickering on the floor of the room.

Heap went to his window on three occasions over a period of two to three hours, watching for nearly an hour on one occasion. He identified the flames on the floor as sulphur burning on plates, an opinion shared by his fellow watchers. They also agreed it was a strange, possibly dangerous, occurrence. Sulphur was used as a disinfectant to fumigate linen or an empty room, never when a patient was in residence.

The men in the infirmary agreed upon another curious thing. For all their observations none of them had seen the sentry passing the infectious ward, something he was required to do every five minutes. Those who should have been asleep, and were not, and became suspicious, wondered over those who should have been awake and suspicious, and apparently were not.

The watchers did not report what they had seen and heard, even when the senior medical officer, Surgeon Major Penrice of the West Norfolk Militia, visited the ward that morning. Penrice saw Smith and made the standard solicitous enquiry of doctor to patient, to which Smith dutifully replied that he was feeling better.

That afternoon, 4 August, Smith complained to the visiting scripture reader, Mr Adie, of ill treatment by the orderlies. Adie passed the complaint to Adjutant Charles Tye. That evening Tye took a statement from Smith. The following day, Brigade Surgeon John Sparrow of the Army Medical Department at Colchester visited Smith and took another statement. The infirmary watchers, now aware of Smith's complaint, admitted their observations.

An inspection of Smith's room showed that the grate of the stove was full of straw, and pieces of straw could be seen in the chimney. Sparrow called for an inventory of sulphur in the store and Sergeant Browne produced two bottles, one obviously long empty because of the dead flies inside, and a second missing two ounces. Sparrow also wanted to know why an earthenware spittoon was missing and Sergeant Browne produced the pieces, retrieved from Smith's room by Pritchard.

The sentries had to be interviewed, a protracted exercise destined to embarrass the Army. Private Robert Agnew, the sentry for 11 pm to 1 am, had seen and heard things, some of which he chose to forget. He did recall seeing Solly, Pritchard and Davies outside Smith's room and hearing Smith call out 'murder' or 'have mercy'. Later Agnew heard Smith shout, 'Go away, go away,' and, seeing Solly and Pritchard at the door of the room, Agnew asked, 'What is up with the man?' After receiving no reply Agnew said, 'Why don't you come away and let the poor fellow die in peace?' Pritchard supposedly muttered something unintelligible in reply.

Agnew made no reference to anything said by Solly, a vital and deliberate omission by a sentry doomed to be discredited, not just for omitting evidence but failing to carry out his duty. Agnew claimed that he did not pass the infectious ward again that night because he did not

(1) THE INFECTIOUS WARD.
(2) THE INFIRMARY.—PRIVATE HEAP WATCHING THE BURNING SULPHUR.

The infirmary, right, depicting the watching Private Heap; a sketch used by the press.

wish to disturb the patient with the noise of his boots and spurs, an explanation that took no account of the grassed area.

The sentry who relieved Agnew at 1 am could also be relevant, and was, but Agnew and the Army between them could not decide the identity of that soldier, the Army confused by subterfuge and conspiracy among its soldiers and Agnew losing his memory in the interest of self-preservation, more of which later.

Private Briscoe performed sentry duty from 3 am and seemingly took refuge from early questioning behind a bout of scarlet fever, though that should not have prevented the Army from talking to him. He would in time throw light on the sentry he relieved, and other matters.

The Army convened a Board of Inquiry, headed by Lieutenant Colonel Curtis, and with commendable speed, notwithstanding some evasive and elusive sentries, decided the events of the night of 3/4 August should be handed over to the civilian authorities. The Mayor, Harry Bullard, and Justices' Clerk, George Kennett, were no less positive and quick in their reaction. Smith was dying and his evidence would go with him unless it was reeled in.

INTERIOR OF THE ROOM IN WHICH SMITH DIED.

Private Smith's room.

On Friday, 6 August 1880, Mayor Bullard and Justices' Clerk Kennett met Brigade Surgeon Sparrow, Adjutant Tye, Sergeant Browne and privates Davies, Solly and Pritchard, in the presence of John Smith, proposing to obtain that rarest of legal documents, a dying declaration. The maker of such a declaration must acknowledge imminent death and John Smith had no illusions. The document is repeated as taken.

The said John Smith, on his oath, saith:

'I was a patient in the hospital at the Barracks on the 3rd of August, 1880. I was in this room at twelve o'clock on that night. I am a private in the 2-17th Regiment of Foot. At twelve o'clock two men, Davies and Solly, now present, came into the room. They told me they were going into the other room. They first shifted my bedside table, and tried to get hold of the sheet off my bed. I shouted and they went out of the room. They came back in two or three minutes, and went and turned the light down. They then put some sulphur at the foot of my bed.

I don't know what it was on. It was burning, and I knew it was
sulphur from the smell. I shouted out, and the patients from the
ward opposite got up at the windows to look. I could see them
because there was a light in their room and I was in darkness.
They went away then and left me two or three hours, and left the
sulphur burning. When they came back in about three hours they
dropped more sulphur on the plate. They then closed the
windows. I hollered out again and threw my spit-cup at the
window. I was helpless and confined to bed from disease and
could not move my body to walk. The spit-cup broke by striking
on the window sill and Pritchard threw away the pieces next
morning. He came into my room first at about six o'clock and
opened the windows and the door. The smoke went out at the top
of the windows. When Davies and Solly came in the second time,
at about half past two to three, Solly put some straw up the
chimney. I forgot to mention that before. When they went out at
that time they shut the door and the windows and left the sulphur
burning. I was almost suffocated by it. But I was stronger the next
day in my talk. In the morning at about half past eight, the three
orderlies – Davies, Solly and Pritchard – came in and gave me a
bath. I told them not to interfere with me until the doctor came.
They put me in a bath against my will and gave me rather a
shorter bath. They did not keep me in so long as usual. They put
me in very steady. They gave me a light bath, and I promised I
would not tell the doctor or sergeant about the night affair. I was
afraid of them. I told Mr Adie the scripture reader of it when I saw
him in the afternoon. He was the first person I had told about it.
He was not the first person I had seen. The straw was taken out of
the chimney the next morning by Pritchard directly after he came
into the room, at about a quarter past six. The orderlies were
always kind to me. I got all my diet regularly, except my fish now
and then. I believe all three – Davies, Solly and Pritchard – have
an interest in taking my life, and Solly in particular. Solly is the
worst. I had left them a few shillings in a bit of a will, and they
knew I had done so. I heard them talking together outside that
night, but I could not hear what they said. I did not hear either of
the sentries that night. The gas was turned down low and I could
not see who brought the sulphur in. I heard Solly say the same
night by my bedside he wished I was out of the way. He said this
to me. I did not report it to the adjutant in the morning when he
visited me. I did not report to him at all. I reported it to Mr Adie,
the scripture reader, in the afternoon, and the adjutant came to
me in the evening about it. I know I am in a very critical state and
I am likely to die very shortly. I have been in the hospital about six
months. I came from Shorncliffe, which is about eight miles from

Dover. I feel perfectly confident about making these statements and that my mind is perfectly clear.'

In response to Sergeant Browne:

'You have visited me to ask me if I have any complaint, but not every day. I have no recollection of the days you have not visited me. You visited me on the night of the occurrence from a quarter to half past ten. You visited me on the morning afterwards, just before the doctor came. I made no complaint to you. I was afraid of the orderlies I told you about a few days ago, that I thought there was a chance I might get rounded [sic]. I never deserted from a militia regiment nor yet from her Majesty's service, but I have been tried for absence without leave.'

Davies did not wish to ask any questions. In response to Pritchard:

'When you came to me on the night of the 3rd you put my shoulders right and my feet. I did not tell you to go away from my bed and that I did not want you any more. I was as wide awake all night long as I am at this present moment. I was not muttering anything about Emma. I have no recollection of the name of Emma. I did tell you on that day I could not see my hand before me.'

In response to Solly:

'I did not tell you in the afternoon that I could not see. You wiped the corner of my eye with a handkerchief. I saw you after the sergeant went out at watch-calling, at about half past ten.'

In response to Mayor Bullard:

'I did not hear anybody but the orderlies out of the room.'

Smith made his mark on his dying declaration that Friday, 6 August, and the mayor convened a magistrates' hearing at the Norwich Guildhall for Monday, 9 August. Private John Smith died on Sunday, 8 August, the cause given as consumption. His evidence had been preserved just in time.

The four soldiers appeared in custody before magistrates under the chairmanship of Mayor Bullard, investigator turned adjudicator. The bench included the deputy mayor and nine other magistrates. Six high-ranking Army officers sat behind the magistrates, headed by the brigade surgeon general. Outside the Guildhall a vociferous and unruly crowd fought to gain entrance, tussling with police as they sought the few places available in the Sword Room. The *Norwich Argus* had learned of the case and issued a special supplement, prompting a siege of its office by a crowd eager for news. At the Guildhall the newspaper reported that the crowd's 'furious and frantic efforts to gain admission' were diverted by 'a woman with dishevelled hair and brutal countenance dragged durance vile by two policemen along St Peter's Street.' Eventually the outside settled, watching and waiting upon any comings and goings, and the inside got down to business.

The defendants were jointly charged with burning sulphur with intent to suffocate and kill John Smith, in other words attempted murder, and, again jointly, with feloniously administering sulphur to endanger Smith's life, a fall-back in case the first charge failed. The *Norwich Argus* thought they were 'the most extraordinary charges of modern times'.

The court had another document to consider. The will of the deceased, made out in his true name of Arthur Hurt. It appears that Hurt had deserted from the Army and rejoined as John Smith, something the Army must have discovered because Surgeon Major Penrice and Adjutant Tye were witnesses to the will, made on 26 July 1880. Hurt, alias Smith, had willed his aunt in Nottingham to receive all his worldly goods, less £1 to William Davies and ten shillings each to William Solly and Henry Pritchard.

Mr Carlos Cooper told the magistrates that he appeared for the four defendants but had not received any instructions, which did not stop him rigorously cross-examining witnesses and making submissions, one of his early objections being the position of Chief Constable Hitchman 'looking full into the face' of witness Agnew. Mayor Bullard quickly dismissed that complaint.

The Town Clerk, Mr Miller, presented the prosecution case, built upon the evidence of the deceased, the window watchers, sentry Private Agnew (the Army were still sorting out who had relieved him) and the findings and observations of Adjutant Tye, Surgeon Major Penrice and Brigade Surgeon Sparrow. Private Turner gave evidence of clearing the chimney a few days previously when no straw existed there or in the stove.

A salient point concerning the evidence that put the three orderlies in the infectious ward that night is that Pritchard, as duty orderly, was the only one entitled to be there. Solly was the infirmary orderly and Davies should not have been in either place on that particular night.

The Town Clerk resorted to asking leading questions of the defensively minded Private Agnew, to which Mr Cooper objected.

Mayor Bullard ruled: 'You must consider his [Agnew's] position – he is trying to screen himself from some other tribunal for neglecting his duty. The Town Clerk has a right to treat him as a hostile witness.'

Mayor Harry Bullard, investigator and adjudicator. Norfolk County Council Library & Information Services

The Town Clerk dragged out Agnew's evidence by comparing his stilted answers with those he had given the Army Board of Inquiry. Agnew said he had forgotten who relieved him on sentry duty but, under cross-examination, he thought it was Private Hewitt, an answer that accorded with Army records if not their inquiries. Agnew neglected to speak of anything said to him by Solly.

Surgeon Major David Penrice told the court that fumigating the ward without his permission was 'an unwarrantable liberty' and if sulphur had been used a report should have been left. His memory faltered on other matters and the Town Clerk used his answers to the Board of Inquiry to remind him, which again upset Mr Cooper. Mayor Bullard ruled: 'The magistrates have decided, Mr Town Clerk, that you may ask this witness any questions you please.' Again Mr Cooper objected. Again the mayor overruled him. Mr Cooper asked that his objection be noted and retired from the fray.

The hearings continued on two successive Saturdays, concluding on 21 August when Mr Cooper addressed the bench, seeking to have the case thrown out. He asked if it was likely that his clients would have conceived the horrible idea of suffocating a patient whose death was daily expected. He said they could have been moving the patient with no desire to do him any harm, resulting in a cry of 'have mercy'. He pointed out that the blinds in the room had not been pulled down despite the orderlies being under the gaze of the infirmary, hardly the actions of men intent upon murder. He said Smith had not mentioned Sergeant Browne and the sentries had not seen him.

The magistrates retired for a quarter of an hour before Mayor Bullard announced that all four men would be committed for trial. Mr Cooper applied for bail on behalf of Browne, saying the case against him was weak. The Town Clerk opposed the application, saying there was strong evidence implicating Browne, and the mayor observed that the fourth

Victim and accused – a press depiction.

man in the room was probably Browne. After more discussion and argument the mayor admitted Browne to bail in a recognisance of £50. His fellow accused were sent back to Norwich Castle.

The case was scheduled for the Winter Assizes before the Lord Chief Justice, Mr Justice Hawkins, but only just scraped past the Grand Jury. They found a true bill only after Mr Justice Hawkins told them he would refrain from opinion but thought 'no adequate motive could be expected to be found'.

At the Assizes trial Mr Blofeld prosecuted and Mr Gates QC appeared for Browne. Mr Carlos Cooper represented the other three accused.

Mr Gates disputed the identification of Browne by Heap and Logan and said that Heap's chequered Army career, including a previous malicious complaint against Sergeant Browne, did not make him a readily believable witness. Heap had joined the Army in 1865 and deserted in 1872, re-enlisting in the 12th Lancers by virtue of a false declaration on oath, a deception duly discovered. Booted out of the Lancers, he had somehow joined the Inniskillings.

The confusion over sentries had finally been resolved, to their detriment. Private Briscoe, recovered from scarlet fever, said he saw Solly, Pritchard and Davies in the room adjoining Smith's room and observed that a rug or blanket had been placed over the door of Smith's room. From the outside he observed that the window was closed and the gaslight turned down. And he had relieved Private Hill, not Private Hewitt!

Agnew now admitted that Private Hill had relieved him, saying he had not previously said so because he (Agnew) would have got into trouble. Evidence was put before the court that the sergeant of the guard had submitted a false return of sentry duties and Private Hewitt, scheduled to relieve Agnew, had earlier undertaken front gate duty. The sentries had been pursuing their own agenda.

The hapless Agnew now spoke of matters he had kept back. Speaking to Solly and Pritchard at the door of Smith's room he had asked 'What's up?' and Solly had replied, according to Agnew, 'The doctor gave an order we were to do away with that man.' This new and riveting evidence prompted the judge to cross-examine Agnew.

Judge: 'You understand, I suppose, that "doing away" meant murdering him?'

Agnew: 'Yes.'

Judge: 'Did you ever hear of a doctor giving an order to murder a man before?'

Agnew: 'No.'

Judge: 'Did it not strike you as a strange order for a doctor to give concerning a man in the hospital?'

Agnew: 'Yes.'

Judge: 'Did you not think it was your duty to report this extraordinary moment?'

Agnew: 'No.'

Judge: 'If you had seen the man being actually murdered you would not have interfered?'

Agnew: 'Oh yes, I should.' He went on to say he did not believe the statement to be true.

The judge offered the view that it was no use asking Agnew any questions.

Private Hill, the unmasked sentry who had kept quiet for two months, gave evidence of seeing the three orderlies in the infectious ward on the night in question and asking Solly what was up, receiving the reply, 'Nothing'. He said he saw earthenware plates in the ward and Davies shaking a 'bluish' bottle. Hill admitted that he had been drinking beer in the company of the orderlies and had not patrolled as he should have done, and a few days earlier he had been arrested by Sergeant Browne for creating a disturbance in the hospital. The sentries would answer to the Army for dereliction of duty and prevarication, but it is more than possible they did not patrol past Smith's room because they knew or suspected what was going on.

Adjutant Tye said that when he first saw Smith about his complaint Smith said he couldn't recognise any of the men who had come into his room on the night of 3 August. Tye said he had in the past seen the chimney of Smith's room stopped up with straw.

Surgeon Major Penrice denied ever giving an order to 'do away' with the patient and said that when he saw Smith in the morning the man not only said he felt better but he'd had a good night. Penrice said that Smith had previously told him the orderlies were 'kind and gentle' but he, Penrice, thought they were 'no more than sufficient'. Penrice admitted he had recently authorised the lighting of a small fire in Smith's room to combat the awful stench in the place and that the condition of the patient was so offensive he had to be moved often, and that took more than one person. He agreed he had authorised Sergeant Browne to use sulphur to fumigate linen. In his opinion Browne was a 'humane and well-conducted man'.

The defence case improved significantly when cross-examination trapped Brigade Surgeon Sparrow into saying that whilst burning sulphur in a patient's room was dangerous the quantity apparently used was unlikely to cause death, especially if the ventilators were open, and it appears they were. He said that Browne had the key to the sulphur store. Sparrow denied that he had threatened Sergeant Browne with arrest if he did not produce the missing spittoon.

The prosecution fought back with a new witness – a prisoner from Norwich Castle. John Sherwood Siggery had been in the cell next to William Davies and they had unseeingly spoken into the corridor through their respective cell apertures, despite a rule that prisoners were not allowed to speak to each other. Siggery's evidence was that Davies came back to his cell crying after a visit from his wife and he asked what ailed the young man.

Davies allegedly replied, 'I think it is all up with us now. I think we shall get ten years; but if I do, it is all through the sergeant. It is not my fault. I think I shall turn Queen's Evidence. I don't think I shall get out of it if I don't.' He went on to say, according to Siggery, 'It was not my fault. The sergeant gave me the stuff and I used it,' and 'The sergeant deserved hanging,' and, obviously prompted by Siggery, 'The sergeant took some stuff out of a new canister or packet and gave it to me and told me if anyone asked who it was for, I was to say it was for someone who wanted brimstone and treacle,' and Smith had called out, 'Oh dear; do not kill me,' and Solly was sure to give Queen's Evidence because he could not stand cross-examination. The sergeant had supposedly said he was going to use soldier B.211 to do the job (a statement to doubt because Private B.211 Johnson had deserted in 1858).

A listening prisoner warned Davies that as he couldn't see whom he was talking to that person could be a policeman, whereupon Davies fainted.

Strangely, Siggery's previous life had included being a policeman. Perhaps retrospective leanings prompted him to seek an interview with the governor or, more likely, he was intent upon ingratiation knowing that in addition to his incarceration for stealing a gallon of potatoes at Winchester he was wanted for stealing lead in Surrey.

The prison governor was not disposed to interview Siggery. He gave him a pen and paper and told him to write down what he wanted to say. That statement now lay before Mr Justice Hawkins and Siggery was called to the witness box to speak to it. Unfortunately he did not speak to it with great accuracy and the judge commented, 'You have not told us the same story today.'

Siggery replied, 'As near as I can remember,' adding, 'We often talked together and he told me many things. I have something else to say.'

The judge said, 'But I can't let you say it unless you are asked.' Siggery was not asked and, although some of what he said had a ring of truth, he was seen as a disreputable witness pursuing his own interests.

Mr Gates said there was no real evidence against Sergeant Browne, none of the sentries had seen him, and as Brigade Surgeon Sparrow's evidence intimated there was no great danger from the sulphur the charge of endangering life must in any case be withdrawn from the jury.

Mr Justice Hawkins said the evidence against Browne was 'very, very slight', observing, 'If there is any evidence at all, it is only a scintilla.'

Mr Blofeld took his cue and began his closing speech by withdrawing the charges against Sergeant Browne. He then submitted that in all probability the other prisoners forgot that the ventilators were open when they burned the sulphur and their intent was 'to hurry a dying man out of the world a few days sooner'. He asked the jury to give credence to Siggery's evidence because he had nothing to gain by making it up, further asking if Smith 'would have invented a diabolical lie when he knew his death was so near?'

Mr Justice Hawkins said the count of administering sulphur to endanger life had been 'negatived'. Mr Cooper therefore addressed only the attempted murder charge and said that if sulphur had been used by the prisoners it would have been to purify and cleanse the room. He pointed out that they were respectable men and had always been kind to Private Smith. He said that Private Agnew had 'studiously avoided divulging material evidence' and no reliability should be placed on anything he said. He likewise dismissed the testimony of Siggery, who had made his statement while awaiting his own trial. He asked the jury to give the prisoners the benefit of the doubts in the case.

Mr Justice Hawkins said it was immaterial to the remaining charge that the sulphur used was insufficient to cause death; the issue was whether the prisoners intended death to result. He queried what their motive might have been and pointed out that there was no evidence that they had expressed the hope that their loathsome duties were at an end or that they were disgusted and dissatisfied, or that they knew of the contents of Smith's will. (The dying declaration said they did know.) In reviewing the evidence the judge made reference to Private Agnew's newly revealed claim that Solly had said the doctor ordered Smith done away with, saying 'notwithstanding the stir made in the city by this occurrence this man had most unaccountably kept his knowledge back'. The value of Siggery as a witness he left to the jury.

The jury retired and soon returned with a verdict of 'Not Guilty' in respect of all three prisoners. Applause rang through the public gallery, quickly hushed by court officials. Mr Justice Hawkins discharged the three men and outside the Shirehall they were greeted by what the *Eastern Daily Press* called 'some demonstration'.

How these four men finished their careers is not known. They and some of the soldier witnesses may have decided their future lay outside the Army; in some cases the Army may have made that decision. William Browne was, however, a career man. He got his promotion: to Sergeant Major at Aldershot.

CHAPTER 8

The New Century

The Yarmouth Beach Murders, 1900 & 1912

Murder fascinates and horrifies, some cases quickly fading into history whilst others long remain in the public eye. The 1900 Yarmouth beach murder has been the subject of articles and books, all broadly agreeing the facts but not concurring upon the identity of the murderer, believed by some to have struck again in 1912. Much has already been written and postulated but theories and facts are now offered under a 21st-century microscope.

In 1900 the police were on the threshold of forensic advances and were more publicly accepted and respected. They were no longer labourers of the magistrates, and were now uniformed by helmets and tunics and supported by plain-clothes officers of a Criminal Investigation Department.

Bathing machines on the beach were a sign of Great Yarmouth's growing status as a holiday resort and fourteen-year-old John Norton was charged with looking after these wheeled contraptions. A little after six o'clock on the morning of 23 September 1900, with the early light promising a fine day, he walked to work along South Beach in an area of marram grass, hillocks and hollows and saw what he thought, firstly, to be a bundle of clothes in the sand, secondly, a sleeping woman. On a closer sighting he recoiled from a dead body.

Norton ran along Marine Parade and found Constable Edwin Manship who, after confirming the tragedy, sent him to find another policeman and a horse and cart. The blue-black complexion of the once-good-looking woman and her stiffened body removed any doubt as to death, and the double-knotted mohair bootlace around her neck showed the manner of her dying. She lay on her back, her skirt raised to her knees, bloomers lowered, her dyed golden hair resting against the sand, her sailor hat nearby with hatpins still neatly in place. The sand had been trampled, more so four yards seaward of the body. Had she struggled and broken free only to be brought down four yards later?

Manship stood by the body making a note – a mental note. He made no sketch or written record at the scene. Preserving the scene did not occur to him.

Norton returned with two constables on a horse-drawn cart. They loaded the sand-spattered body onto the cart, trampling over the already trampled sand, and set off for the mortuary. The beach was left to the public disporting themselves as they chose.

A search of the body at the mortuary gave the first signs of the mystery to come. The dead woman wore a wedding ring but had nothing upon her body or clothes that might identify her. Police Surgeon Thomas Lettis thought death had occurred between one and two o'clock in the morning. A post-mortem by Lettis and Dr Charles O'Farrell confirmed death from asphyxia caused by the bootlace ligature. Lettis found marks that he tentatively attributed to attempted rape, later becoming even less sure. Her fingernails showed no sign of fighting for her life but her face had been faintly scratched and there were slight bruises on her lip and jaw. Possibly she was the author of her disarranged clothing, after which sudden violence had overtaken her.

Edward Fish, a resident of the famous Yarmouth rows, provided the first clue to where the dead woman had come from, if not her identity. He stopped on an early morning errand to gossip with a patrolling policeman, as people used to do, and mentioned that a young woman lodger of his neighbours had scandalously stayed out all night. The

police quickly took John Rudrum of No 3, Row 104 (Custom House Row) to the mortuary, where he identified the stay-out lodger.

The young woman had taken lodgings with Mrs Eliza Rudrum just before nine o'clock on the evening of Saturday, 15 September. She had worn new clothes, carried a small suitcase and paper parcel, and been accompanied by a child she introduced as Rosie, aged two years. She did not give her own name but said she had just arrived by train from London having travelled from York, where she lived. She said she had been a widow for two years and Mrs Rudrum had been recommended by a 'friend's friend'. She paid for a week's lodging saying her brother-in-law had travelled with her and she

The victim lodged in Row 104, Custom House Row. A fragment remains today.
Colin Tooke

would go and see him before he returned to London. After putting her daughter to bed she left the house. The fact that the brother-in-law was not present assisting with the child and luggage, and there were no more trains to London that night, may have struck Mrs Rudrum as odd.

Near midnight, when the new lodger had failed to return, John Rudrum stepped outside to look for her and almost immediately saw her entering the row in the company of a man. He stepped back and was unable to describe the man. When the young woman came into the house she was a little tipsy. She said that her brother-in-law had treated her to a brandy and fish supper and because he had missed the last train he was now staying in a hotel.

In the week that followed, the nameless lodger went out each day, all day, and on the Wednesday she and her child were photographed by a beach photographer. She proudly showed the picture to Mrs Rudrum. Never was there to be a more important beach photograph.

On the Thursday the young woman told Mrs Rudrum she was expecting a letter and her name became an issue for the first time. She said she was 'Mrs Hood'. She also told Mrs Rudrum that whether she stayed another week depended upon her receiving money from her brother-in-law, which the landlady thought curious because she had seen several sovereigns in her purse.

Mrs Rudrum's 22-year-old daughter, Alice, was certainly curious, suspicious even, concerning their lodger. Mrs Hood had told her she was twenty-six years of age, but informed her mother she was twenty-seven (she was twenty-three). And the journey from York changed to one from Leeds, both false. She said she played the piano and violin and had recently returned from South Africa, both facts disbelieved by the Rudrums but both true.

The letter arrived on the Friday in a bluish envelope addressed to 'Mrs Hood'. The keen-eyed Alice noted the postmark as 'Woolwich'. Alice's observations went further. Retiring to her bedroom in the late evening, she opened the window and saw Mrs Hood talking to a man in the row, just a few yards from No 3. Again there is no description; the man was hidden by darkness and an archway. Alice heard the man gruffly say, 'You understand, don't you? I am placed in an awkward position just now.' Alice withdrew her head and did not hear a reply. She did, however, hear a loud kiss.

When Mrs Hood entered the house Mrs Rudrum handed her the letter. It was quickly opened, Mrs Hood remarking as she read that she had a meeting the next evening 'under the big clock', which she supposed was the Town Hall, agreed by Mrs Rudrum. Mrs Hood then said she would be staying another week. In fact she had but a short time to live.

Mrs Hood left her lodgings at six-thirty on the last evening of her life, smartly dressed and wearing her sailor hat, saying she may be late back. She was, however, back at eight-thirty, by which time only Mrs

A fateful meeting took place 'under the big clock': the Town Hall. Norfolk County Council Library & Information Services

Rudrum's aged mother was in the house. After quickly visiting her room the young woman left, telling Mrs Rudrum's mother she had to see her brother-in-law. She never returned but Alice Rudrum, obviously prying, saw her waiting outside the Town Hall at nine o'clock and exchanged pleasantries before passing on. Mrs Hood was not seen alive again, not for certain.

Alfred Mason, aged nineteen years, and Blanche Smith, aged seventeen years, sought to take advantage of the darkness and a warm night and went onto the South Beach, selecting a secluded hollow for privacy. At a time they estimated to be between eleven and eleven-thirty that privacy was interrupted by the shadowy shapes of another couple treading through the sand, arguing as they passed. They settled about thirty yards away. Within a short time Alfred and Blanche heard the woman moaning and crying 'Mercy! Mercy!' There followed more moans and then silence. The young couple, embarrassed and unsure of themselves, got up and walked from the beach, passing within a few yards of the other couple. Their sidelong glances observed the woman lying on her back with her skirt above her knees, the man crouching over her. He turned his face towards the passing couple but neither Alfred nor

Blanche could penetrate the darkness to make out his features. They hurried away. Alfred later said he thought the couple were 'skylarking'.

Next morning Alfred Mason heard of the discovery of a body on the beach and went anxiously to Middlegate Street Police Station. Chief Constable William Parker interviewed him and ordered officers to find Blanche Smith and take her to the South Beach to point out the exact spot where the other couple had been seen. This she did, losing the evidential value because the officers pointed to the murder spot and asked if that was the one. Then it got worse. Blanche said she wasn't sure.

Detective Inspector Robert Lingwood searched the deceased woman's room and found the beach photograph. He also found the return half of a rail ticket from Liverpool Street Station dated 15 September but not the Woolwich letter. Mrs Rudrum told him that her lodger wore a long gold chain and silver watch around her neck. There had been no gold chain and silver watch on the body. Alice Rudrum had no doubt that Mrs Hood had been wearing her watch and chain outside the Town Hall. Clothing in the room was not marked but the child's clothes had the laundry mark 599.

Great Yarmouth police made the local inquiries a modern police force would make, visiting hotels and boarding-houses, checking the railway station, interviewing cabbies, traders and the like. The beach photograph was sent to other police forces along with photographs taken in the mortuary by a local photographer, Frank Sayers, a pioneering use of photographs in a murder investigation. The laundry mark was not deemed worthy of national circulation. The London rail ticket should have made it a priority.

Foot-slogging inquiries continued and a police visit to the *Crown and Anchor* hotel at Hall Quay became just another negative in a long list of negatives. Later it would be a positive.

A visit to the *Mariner's Compass* at South Quay proved fruitful. The landlord, William Borking, thought the murdered woman had been in his bar between half past nine and ten o'clock on the Saturday evening, accompanied by a man wearing a grey suit. He claimed

Detective Inspector Robert Lingwood.
Paul Capon

he had preserved the glasses used by the couple – presumably as trophies because fingerprint expertise was several years away from the Great Yarmouth police. Borking, largely built, heavily bearded and noisily larger than life, had a keen financial eye and was a friend of John Rudrum, himself now basking in press attention.

John Headley had an interest as a newsagent and local representative of a national newspaper. At seven o'clock on the Sunday morning he had waited at Yarmouth's Southtown railway station to collect newspapers, noticing a young man, slightly built with a slight moustache, dressed in a grey suit and dark trilby, standing at the door of a first-class compartment of the seven-twenty train to Liverpool Street. The man appeared to be nervously waiting for a companion but nobody came and he boarded the train.

On the Wednesday after the murder a Lowestoft newsagent reported circumstances that instantly fitted the crime. John O'Driscoll said that at nine o'clock that morning an agitated man with scratches on his face had demanded a newspaper with the best report of the Yarmouth murder. In serving the man he noticed scratches on his hand and saw the tongue of his boot was protruding, as if the bootlace was missing. The man trembled as he opened the newspaper and read the report. He then ran from the shop. O'Driscoll described him as wearing a long grey overcoat, well spoken, in his twenties with a heavy moustache. A red herring? Probably, but at that time the bootlace had not been mentioned in the press.

The inquest on 27 September heard from various witnesses to Mrs Hood's short time in Great Yarmouth and to the discovery of her body and the extent of police inquiries. The coroner severely criticised Constable Manship for moving the body and didn't like the way he gave his evidence either. The chief constable did not offer an early conclusion to the case and the hearing was adjourned. Mrs Hood was buried in Yarmouth cemetery in a simple coffin marked 'unknown', with 'Hood' in brackets. The mourners were few but included the Rudrums and Detective Inspector Lingwood.

The case needed an injection of new thinking, a second trawl of available evidence and new lines of inquiry. The chief constable sought the assistance of Scotland Yard (formed in 1878). This in a modern light might seem something he should have done earlier but, although provincial forces did sometimes seek the assistance of the Metropolitan Police, the Home Secretary did not formally approve the practice until 1908. Later there came ground rules, or at least an understanding that calling in the Yard should come early in the investigation, not after the local force had thrashed around for three weeks and got nowhere. It is likely that Chief Constable Parker's request was not welcomed, and he probably only made it after local pressure; nevertheless, Detective Chief Inspector Alfred Leach of Scotland Yard was assigned to the case.

Leach saw the importance of the laundry mark (it was said he didn't know about it until a newspaper reporter told him) and instituted inquiries to trace it in York, Leeds and London, particularly Woolwich. He also picked up on the reference to South Africa and ordered an examination of passenger lists sailing to that country. In two strokes he would achieve the breakthrough, demonstrating that a parochial investigation has limitations.

The laundry mark achieved success without that success at first being noticed. It was traced to a laundry at Bexley Heath (Bexleyheath) and a Mrs Bennett, but she was apparently still sending her linen to the laundry. A detective reported a negative. He didn't know the laundry now came from Mr Bennett.

Detective work is rarely blinding flashes of inspiration and intuition, more painstaking and lengthy inquiries into small facets of information. The detective allocated the shipping lists worked through records for 1900 probably hoping he would not be faced with 1899 or before. He found that on 17 March 1900 a Mr and Mrs Hood sailed from Southampton to Cape Town, arriving on 10 April; and a Mr and Mrs Hood sailed from Cape Town four days later, arriving in England on 9 May. The detective found a shipping clerk who remembered the Hoods arriving from Cape Town with the name Bennett on their luggage. The booking record of the outgoing Hoods showed cash had been paid and the banknotes had been recorded. A bank at Westgate-on-Sea had issued them to a Mr Bennett. The Hoods, alias Bennetts, had spent only four days in South Africa.

Leach ordered a new inquiry into Mrs Bennett at Bexley Heath and this time the laundry manager identified his customer from the beach photograph. Mrs Bennett, and husband and child, had lived in rented accommodation, where she had been known to some as Mrs Bartlett, and to others as Mrs Good. Mr Bartlett, or Good, or Bennett, had rarely been seen, said by his wife to be a commercial traveller. Identifying Mrs Hood as Mrs Bennett was as good as it got for the time being. She had moved.

The police found that Herbert John Bennett had married Mary Jane Clark in July 1897. Mary had been a music teacher (piano and violin) and Herbert had been her pupil – and more, because she became pregnant, and in consequence they married. When registering the marriage Herbert gave his age as twenty-four (he was seventeen) and said his father was dead (he was alive). Herbert was regularly a stranger to the truth.

The child that had prompted the marriage had been stillborn. The Bennett's second child, a daughter named Ruby, now in Yarmouth under the pseudonym of Rosie, had been born in 1898. In the years 1897 to 1900 the Bennetts stayed in lodgings and rented accommodation in several places in and around London, Herbert working as a shop assistant and greengrocer. Their finances improved when Mary bought violins wholesale and sold them under false names from accommodation

Herbert John Bennett and Mary Jane Bennett. Yarmouth Independent

addresses. She advertised each violin as the property of a deceased professor, purporting to be his destitute widow. Herbert further bolstered their income by obtaining goods on credit and selling them, quickly moving on, known then and now as long-firm fraud. Herbert dodged creditors while Mary avoided dissatisfied violin customers.

Herbert purchased a greengrocer's shop at Westgate-on-Sea and eight days later it caught fire. After drawing the insurance and leaving Rosie with a relative, buying wigs and a false moustache and telling people he was going to America, he fled with Mary to South Africa under the name of Hood.

Herbert Bennett separated from his wife in June 1900 and moved into lodgings in Union Street, Woolwich. He worked as a Co-op shop assistant and in July obtained employment at Woolwich Arsenal. In October he rented a room in nearby Williams Street. This was either a bolthole or another address from which to run some fraudulent enterprise.

The London newspapers had reported the murder of Mrs Hood in detail, and did so again when the inquest concluded on 29 October with a verdict of murder by person or persons unknown.

Herbert Bennett's downfall came through a piano and bicycle. He sold them to a colleague, Robert Allen, who made enquiries and found he had been misled, in fact cheated. On 6 November Allen met Bennett outside the Woolwich Arsenal gates on the pretence of seeking redress for a piano and bicycle. As they walked and talked, Detective Chief Inspector Leach and Detective Sergeant Holford barred their way. Allen introduced 'Mr Bennett' and stepped aside, his role completed. There was no polite police request to assist with inquiries. Leach brusquely identified himself, told Bennett he was under arrest for the murder of Mrs Hood, ignored the startled protest and, with the additional clamping hands of Holford, hustled him into a waiting cab. Chief Constable Parker and Detective Inspector Lingwood waited at Woolwich Police Station.

Ruby, alias 'Rosie', Bennett.
Great Yarmouth Library

Bennett fiercely claimed his innocence. The police were not impressed. They saw a smartly dressed, slightly built young man looking older than his years by virtue of a faint moustache with waxed ends, and knew they had detained a confidence trickster and prime suspect for murder, but they needed a motive for the murder. Bennett gave them one. He asked if Alice Meadows, a parlour maid at Bayswater, could be informed of his arrest. Alice Meadows was his fiancée.

Constable Elliston of the Metropolitan Police went to Woolwich Police Station, steered there after his wife had hesitated over the beach photograph, and identified Bennett as lodging at the Elliston house in Plumstead with Mrs Bennett in May and June. Mrs Elliston would speak of a fractious relationship between the Bennetts and overhearing an argument in which Bennett shouted at his wife, 'I wish you were dead and if you are not careful you soon will be!' Mrs Bennett had, according to Mrs Elliston, replied, 'If you don't look out I shall send you into penal servitude for fifteen years.'

Bennett told interviewing officers that he had never been to Great Yarmouth. Alice Meadows, of whom the police had no knowledge until he mentioned her, would put him in Great Yarmouth.

Things got even better for the police. Visiting Bennett's Union Street address they found bluish envelopes and learned of his rooms at Williams Street, where they found wigs and a false moustache, a receipt from the *Crown and Anchor* hotel in Great Yarmouth dated the August Bank Holiday, a rent receipt for yet another London address and a gold chain with a silver watch. Incredulous possibility grew to near-certainty as the watch and chain were dangled before Bennett. He trembled, remained silent, thinking furiously before snapping out 'She has not worn that for over twelve months.' Confirmation!

Alice Meadows went to Woolwich Police Station and learned that her fiancé was a married man with a child, and presents of jewellery and clothes that 'Bert' had recently given her, significantly since the death of

Mrs Hood, belonged to his wife. The August Bank Holiday receipt for the *Crown and Anchor* related to Alice and Bert holidaying together in Great Yarmouth, in separate rooms.

Chief Constable Parker and Detective Inspector Lingwood escorted Bennett to Great Yarmouth and, cognisant of the publicity surrounding the arrest, deliberately misled the press upon the time of arrival. A large crowd welling around Yarmouth Southtown Station had dispersed when they eventually arrived.

In the midst of great newspaper publicity concerning Bennett's arrest Mrs Rudrum recalled a letter in that name asking for rooms for the Bank Holiday weekend. She found it, dated 30 July, in the same handwriting, she said, as the Woolwich letter, and it was from Bennett at his Union Street address. She had replied saying she was full up. Alice Rudrum took the letter to Middlegate Street Police Station and was ushered into the chief constable's office and shown the gold watch and chain. She unhesitatingly identified them as those worn by Mrs Hood. She said the child used to bite the watch and her teeth marks should be on the back. The chief constable looked. The teeth marks were there.

On 9 November Bennett appeared before Yarmouth magistrates charged with the murder of Mary Jane Bennett. He said he was not guilty and wanted to make a statement. He was advised against it.

Inquiries at the *Crown and Anchor* to corroborate the August Bank Holiday receipt found a waiter, Walter Reade, who remembered the man staying there the holiday weekend, as per the receipt, and again on 15 September and 22 September. And Reade remembered that on 22 September the man arrived fifteen minutes before midnight in a breathless state, as if he had been running. The man said he was in Yarmouth on business and would leave next morning on the 7.20 am train. The hotel boots, Edward Goodrum, remembered the breathless man arriving and saying he had missed the last tram from Gorleston and had to run to get to the hotel before it closed. The hotel records were incomplete and the man's name could not be found.

Goodrum did not profess to recognise the man again but Reade went to an identification parade arranged by the police and identified Bennett from a line of five men. He knew two of the men previously and Bennett's picture had been blazoned over the newspapers, so he was well on his way to getting it right. John Headley, who had seen the man boarding the 7.20 train, said he would not take the responsibility of viewing the parade.

William Borking of the *Mariner's Compass* had no difficulty picking out Bennett but whilst records show him as a positive witness there is a suggestion that he aimed for fame and fortune from the case and may have been in league with John Rudrum, who was claiming custody of Ruby Bennett, a claim possibly influenced by donations from a sympathetic public: all the inquest jurymen had donated their fee.

The case against Bennett was circumstantial but p*rima facie* good enough, unless he had an alibi for two weekends in September. He did not admit being in Great Yarmouth on either weekend; the August Bank Holiday he now had to admit. He said that on 22 September (the night of the murder) he had been drinking in London with friends William Parritt and James Cameron. He hadn't. That had been on 29 September and Parritt and Cameron would remember accordingly.

From 25 August to 15 September Bennett had been absent from work, recorded as 'sick'. Part of this time he was holidaying in Ireland with Alice Meadows. They were back by 11 September and Bennett was telling his drinking friends that Mary and the child had died of fever in South Africa.

Mary, at a new address in Bexley Heath, had indeed fallen ill in August. When she recovered she told her neighbour, Mrs Langman, she was going on holiday to Yorkshire and 'my old man is going to take me'. Her 'old man' visited her on Friday, 14 September, and gave her money for new clothes, which she bought later that day. Next morning Mary received a telegram, the contents of which she did not disclose. That afternoon Mrs Langman accompanied her to Liverpool Street, a station that does not connect with Yorkshire, and saw her into the station just before 3 pm, never to see her again.

Herbert Bennett saw Alice Meadows on Friday, 14 September and cancelled an arrangement to take her out the next day. He said his grandfather in Gravesend was ill and he would have to go to him. Bennett's grandfather was not ill and he didn't see his grandson that weekend. Just before 3 pm Alice Meadows received a telephone call at her place of work from Bennett to say that he might not be able to see her on the Sunday. Telephones were not common but Alice's well-to-do employers had one, and they could be found at railway stations.

Bennett was missing from his Union Street lodgings over the night of 15/16 September (the night of Mary Bennett's arrival in Yarmouth), appearing on the morning of 16 September at the home of Alice Meadows in Stepney. She was not there and he spoke to her mother and sister before leaving. The 7.20 am train from Great Yarmouth, the first of the morning, had arrived at Liverpool Street at 11.47 am, seventeen minutes late. Alice's home was an estimated two miles from the station. Alice's mother and sister thought Bennett arrived at about 11.30 am. Could they have been wrong?

The following Saturday, 22 September, Bennett's landlady, the beautifully named Mrs Comfort Pankhurst, saw him in the afternoon dressed in a grey suit and bowler hat reading a railway timetable, his interest confirmed when he said he had a train to catch. Mrs Pankhurst thought her lodger to be a nice, quiet young man. She also thought he was single because he had told her so; he had also told her he had a cousin and baby living in Bexley Heath. Mrs Pankhurst didn't see Bennett again that day or night. Once again his bed was not slept in and once again he missed breakfast.

Bennett turned up on the Sunday morning in Hyde Park, near to Alice's place of employment, at about 12.45 pm, still wearing his grey suit and bowler, and 'bumped into' Alice. She declared her surprise, supposing him to again be with his sick grandfather. He said there were too many relatives visiting the old man and he had therefore left. He declined her invitation to dinner, saying he had to go to Woolwich, and walked away. Purpose achieved? On this Sunday morning the Great Yarmouth train into Liverpool Street (seen by Headley) was only one minute late, arriving at 11.31 am.

Committal proceedings before Yarmouth magistrates took place on 16 and 24 November, and finally on 1 December. The courtroom and outside area were crowded on each occasion. Bennett, now represented by a Kent solicitor, Mr Elvy Robb, listened attentively to witnesses and occasionally made notes. The prosecution started badly when William Clark, Mary's grandfather, not only failed to identify the watch and chain he had given her after her grandmother's death but said it wasn't the one. Then Mrs Susan Cato from Balham, Bennett's landlady in late 1899, said there had been two watch-and-chains, and the baby had bitten both of them.

The evidence of Dr Lettis on the question of attempted rape could be termed a fence-sitting example of possibilities but before he gave it the magistrates ordered women from the court. On this issue of sexual assault, nobody seems to have considered the possibility that if Mary had been murdered by her husband he might have wanted to leave the body looking as if a stranger had fallen upon her for sexual purposes. The doctor's timing of death was not queried, evidence not in accord with the young couple's observations on the beach and the breathless man arriving at the *Crown and Anchor*.

Alice Meadows spent two and a half hours in the witness box before fainting. She was carried from the courtroom, the one time Bennett lost some composure.

William Parritt and John Cameron destroyed his alibi for 22 September saying they had not seen him on that date. Parritt fainted in the witness box, recovered and left the courtroom weeping.

William Borking, the *Mariner's Compass* landlord, got in a muddle over his description of the man in his bar and whilst he again identified Bennett it was a buffoon's performance. His washerwoman, Elizabeth Gibson, said she recognised Bennett in the dock as the man who had been in her employer's establishment on the evening in question. She said her recognition was based on the way he twirled his moustache. This simple-minded woman made no better impression than her employer.

Bennett was duly committed for trial at the Norfolk Assizes, the prosecution case weaker than it had been.

In January Mrs Rudrum took a petticoat into the police station pointing to the name 'Bennet' inked onto the garment. She said that after the police search of Mrs Hood's room she had noticed it hanging on the door and had put it away and only now remembered it. Examination of the misspelt name showed the writing to be in ordinary ink, which would have run at the first wash. As Mary Bennett never marked her other clothes and would not in any case have used ordinary ink, and knew how to spell her name, and Detective Inspector Lingwood was adamant the petticoat had not been on the door when he searched the room, the police took a jaundiced view of this 'new evidence', wondering over the motives of the Rudrum family.

Elvy Robb applied to the Law Lords for the case to be removed from Norfolk on the grounds of prejudice fostered by excessive and exaggerated publicity. He said the people of Norfolk had already made up their minds and a fair trial was impossible – a perverse statement with the London newspapers in sensational full cry. The Law Lords accepted Robb's submission. Bennett would be tried at the Old Bailey, at that time a small, suffocating gas-lit building next to Newgate Prison.

Elvy Robb secured the services of the formidable defence advocate Edward Marshall Hall. The presiding judge, Lord Chief Justice Alverstone, would be overseeing his first murder trial and on 25 February 1901 it would be the first murder trial of the twentieth century. Mr Charles Gill prosecuted for the Crown.

The trial lasted six days, during which Bennett remained composed and attentive, if drawn and at times worried. Marshall Hall and Elvy Robb always claimed they were convinced of their client's innocence.

This time grandfather Clark positively identified the watch and chain. Confusion came from the beach photographer, James Conyers, describing Mary in different clothes and wearing a rope chain. Marshall

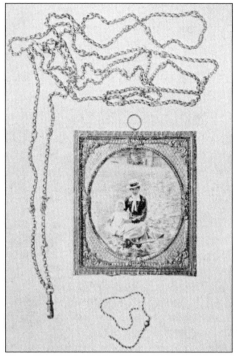

Exhibits: the chain, necklace and beach photograph. Paul Capon

Hall triumphantly produced the exhibit watch on a link chain. Conyers tried to change his mind, too late. Marshall Hall's persistent questioning reduced Mrs Elliston of Plumstead to tears. Her evidence did not accord with interviews and comments she had made to a London newspaper and he showed her to be revelling in her position of a policeman's wife in a major crime case. Having shattered her nerve Marshall Hall scornfully deemed her recollection of the overheard argument between the Bennetts as worthless. As she subsided in confusion he curtly told her tears were the common refuge of her sex.

Mrs Susan Cato, the Balham landlady, fared little better. She told the jury there were definitely two watch-and-chains, both bitten by the baby, but agreed she had not given this information to the police. She admitted she had not only given several press interviews on the case but had written to a London newspaper offering exclusive information for payment, and had been paid. In agreeing these facts she trembled and had to take a glass of water. Her credibility had collapsed.

Miss Elizabeth Langman, daughter of the Bexley Heath neighbour, identified Mary Bennett's clothes, bought to go on holiday, and burst into tears when Marshall Hall contemptuously called her evidence glib. On this occasion the judge reproved him and spoke comfortingly to Miss Langman.

Marshall Hall accused John Rudrum of posing as an important witness to the press and enjoying the fame from his involvement. Rudrum agreed that it was the great event of his life. His wife restored prosecution confidence by speaking of a link chain as opposed to a rope chain, but then undermined the prosecution case by saying Mrs Hood's chain had links longer than the one produced in court. She then changed her mind and said the chain produced was the one worn by Mrs Hood. Marshall Hall tried to change her mind on her description of the bluish envelope addressed to Mrs Hood, and her comparison of the handwriting with the July letter from Bennett, but she refused to budge from her original evidence.

Alice Rudrum gave her evidence firmly without giving ground to

Herbert Bennett in the dock.

Marshall Hall but at the end collapsed into hysterics and had to be
carried screaming and crying from
the court.

William Borking made as poor an
impression as before; more so when
he agreed that he had posed for his
portrait and had his bar photographed for the press.

The evidence from the *Crown and
Anchor* became discredited because
of missing records, and Reade's identification of Bennett was devalued by
the widespread publication of the
arrested man's picture. John
Headley, the newsagent on the railway platform, thought that Bennett
looked like the man he saw getting onto the seven-twenty train.

In the long procession of witnesses there came a new one, a defence
witness giving startling evidence. Sholto Douglas was the respectable
owner of a London manufacturing company and he came forward to say
that at almost four o'clock on the afternoon of 22 September, near
Eltham, a man asked him for a light. He handed over a box of matches,
watched the man light a cigarette (Bennett was a heavy cigarette smok-
er) and walked with the man to a public house, where they had a drink
together. As they left the public house the man pointed to a barber's shop
and spoke of his namesake. The name over the shop was 'Bennett'. The
men shook hands and parted at about seven o'clock, too late to travel to
Great Yarmouth.

Elvy Robb took Douglas to Norwich Prison and showed him Bennett
through the peephole of the cell door. Douglas was sure: that was the
man. Bennett, questioned by Robb, said he recalled the meeting, yet he
could give no confirming detail. In the witness box Sholto Douglas cut
an impressive figure, giving his evidence confidently and resisting Mr
Gill's suggestion of a flawed memory.

During the trial Marshall Hall and Lord Alverstone criticised the
press. Marshall Hall, in his closing speech, called them 'outrageous
gutter-rags', saying their hounding of witnesses and overall sensational-
ism had made the prosecution case unbelievable. He called the police
'violent partisans intent only on winning a show case'. He urged the jury
to a verdict of 'Not Guilty'.

Mr Gill said that Bennett's mysterious absences from London had never been adequately explained, a theme taken up by Lord Alverstone in his two-hour review of the evidence. Marshall Hall was to call it 'a deadly summing up'. The jury retired for thirty-five minutes and returned to deliver a verdict of 'Guilty', received without emotion by Bennett.

Lord Alverstone's sentencing speech was short. Bennett replied to the death sentence with 'I say I am not guilty, sir,' his first words in the trial. Marshall Hall had not sought to place him in the witness box, a twentieth-century innovation that was a double-edged sword because it allowed cross-examination. Bennett was committed to Newgate and subsequently to Norwich to await execution.

Alice Meadows fainted when she heard the verdict and said, 'I will not say that I think him innocent, because there are such a many black incidents against him.' Curiously, she then said she believed Sholto Douglas.

Marshall Hall, having done his best for his client, could have drawn his fee and looked for fresh fields to conquer. Instead he worked tirelessly for a reprieve, obtaining interviews with the Lord Chief Justice and the Home Secretary to press his case. He failed. Bennett's failure to adequately explain his whereabouts on the relevant Saturdays damned him. There would be no reprieve. Marshall Hall wrote to Bennett advising there was no hope and wished him peace in his world to come.

Bennett was to hang at Norwich prison on 21 March 1901, only the second to do so at this prison (George Watt in 1898, see *Norwich Murders*, had been the first). He spent his waiting time in moods varying between sullen silence and violent temper, railing against prison regulations and guarding warders, shouting his innocence. He had no visitors and wrote no letters.

At two minutes to nine on a sunny but bitterly cold morning, an icy wind playing around the austere walls of the prison, the High Sheriff, Major Jary, went into Bennett's cell with the father-and-son executioners James and Thomas Billington. Bennett tersely said he had nothing to say. The Billingtons pinioned him and warders supported him as he walked in the usual procession of officials, chaplain and press to the execution room. The *Yarmouth Independent* described him as 'ghastly pale' and 'semi-fainting'. In a swift fluid movement the Billington team positioned Bennett on the trapdoor, dropped a black cloth and noose over his head and sprang the trapdoor. Witnesses to the execution spoke of Bennett struggling for up to two minutes before remaining still, but the inquest that followed accepted medical evidence that he had died instantly. Herbert Bennett was buried next to George Watt in the prison grounds.

Small groups of spectators stood outside the prison waiting for the formal notice of execution to be posted, silently watching as the black flag ran up the prison flagpole, prompted to sudden exclamation as the flagpole snapped. Flag and pole fell upon the roof of the prison, seen by many as unrelated to the gusting wind but proof that an innocent man had been hanged.

Ruby Bennett had been orphaned, as much a victim as her mother. She was taken into the care of Herbert Bennett's father and the *Sun* newspaper launched a public subscription with a donation of twenty guineas. One wonders what kind of life she made for herself in the twentieth century. A memorial stone was placed on her mother's grave; perhaps she later visited.

A century later the innocence or otherwise of Herbert Bennett remains arguable. He was undeniably a crook, as was his wife, both probably involved in some fraudulent enterprise up to the time of her death. One of the most exhaustive studies of this case came in 1965 from Paul Capon (*The Great Yarmouth Mystery*) and he speculates they may have been conducting a blackmailing scheme, Mary enticing and Herbert threatening. Entirely feasible! Capon concluded that Herbert Bennett 'was almost certainly innocent' of the murder of his wife. Those who believed in Bennett's innocence, whether influenced by the known facts, intuition or a snapped flagpole, received some support in July 1912 with the death of Dora May Gray.

★★★

In the improving light of 4.30 am on Monday, 15 July 1912, William Smith and David Docwra struggled to break-in a horse alongside Yarmouth's South Beach, their efforts held by the sight of a body in the sand just six feet from the road. It was a young woman, clearly strangled. They fetched Police Sergeant Herring to the scene and he, unlike his predecessor in 1900, touched nothing but sent for the chief constable and police surgeon. The exact spot would be measured at 290 yards south of the Nelson Monument, a significant distance from Mary Bennett's place.

The woman, wearing a faded straw hat trimmed with pink roses, smartly costumed in blue, lay on her back with her long plaited hair trailing in the sand, her face contorted and disfigured with blood and froth from her nose and mouth, her tongue protruding and black. Her arms lay by her sides and her bare legs were slightly raised. Her shoes stood at her side, one missing its lace, which was now tightly wound round her neck. Her black cotton stockings, inside out as if pulled off, were also wound round her neck. Slight scratches and abrasions were visible on and under her chin. She had been throttled by the lace from her shoe, her constricting stockings an act of making sure.

Constable Dix drove an ambulance to recover the body and stopped 280 yards short of where it lay as he spotted a pair of gloves lying on the pavement. They would be identified as belonging to the victim.

Identification of the victim came quickly. Dora May Gray, inevitably known as 'Dolly' after the Boer War marching song, had been eighteen

South Beach in 2006. An amusement park has risen above where Mary Jane Bennett was found, bottom. Dora May Gray lay in an area still relatively remote, top, and may have died elsewhere. Mike Page

years of age and had barely known her mother (she had run away when Dora was a child) and never her father. She lived with her aunt, Miss Selina Eastick, and a Miss Brookes, in Manby Road and worked as a seasonal domestic at another address in that road. Her failure to return that night was a first and her aunt feared and realised the worst when she heard of a body on the beach. Her aunt had last seen her at 7.30 pm on the Sunday evening when she left the house saying she was going for a walk.

Dolly, as we shall know her, had been seen by William Bacon at 7.45 that evening on Marine Parade arm-in-arm with a man described as about twenty years of age, dark, six feet tall, wearing a grey suit, slouch hat and brown boots. Near this time Dolly spoke to pier attendant John Harris,

A faded picture but good enough to give an impression of a happy, zestful girl – 'Dolly' Gray.

DORA MAY GRAY.

who described the man in her company as thirty to forty years of age, fair, five-feet-seven to five-feet-eight tall, wearing a grey suit, straw hat and carrying a cane and gloves. They were not arm-in-arm. The last sighting, around 8.45 pm, still on Marine Parade, by her friend Emily Blyth, describes her male companion as aged about twenty years and wearing a grey suit.

Thomas Lettis and Henry Blake carried out the post-mortem and confirmed death from asphyxia, reporting that she was sexually unsullied, though Lettis was as non-committal as he had been with Mary Bennett. He declined to give an opinion upon the scratches and abrasions but Blake was more positive. He said the marks were signs of a brief resistance quickly stifled by the throttling lace from her shoe.

Inquiries soon established that Dolly appeared to have an infatuation with the occupants of yachts tied up at the yacht station. Recently she had spent nearly all day on a yacht, only leaving at four-thirty in the afternoon when the yacht left its moorings. And she had been seen walking on North Quay with yachtsmen and had spoken to the yacht station attendant of going to Lowestoft with a gentleman and meeting that gentleman again in Yarmouth. The attendant, thirteen-year-old Hubert Baldry, commended by the coroner for the way he gave his evidence, said she had regularly called at the station.

As well as at the yacht station, Dolly had been seen on different occasions with different men on Marine Parade and in the vicinity of the Britannia Pier, seemingly a flighty and happy young woman. A letter she received at her place of work, postmarked 'Fakenham', sent the police to that town, where they traced a young man who, like others, had flirted with her. They ruled him out of the inquiry. Inquiries among the Rifle Brigade camped at North Denes also came to nothing.

On 23 July a young man walked into Southend Police Station and admitted murdering Dolly. He was arrested, interviewed and ejected from the station. He was not the only one to confess. The writer of a postcard to Yarmouth police, postmarked 'Tipton', admitted the murder and finished by saying he was now 'well across the water'. A letter-writer from Clapham admitted the murder and advised that his 'guilty memory' compelled him to throw himself into the Thames opposite Cleopatra's Needle. Symbolic or not, a relevant body was not found. Later in the year one of Dolly's boyfriends would confess but, as we shall see, the police sought to prove innocence as much as guilt.

They buried Dolly in Caister cemetery on 26 July 1912. Mourners were pitifully few, reflecting the sad demise of an unwanted child growing up and seeking friendship and dying without evidence of it.

The inquest, twice adjourned, concluded on 31 July. By a strange quirk a member of the jury had been a member of the Mary Bennett inquest jury. After a verdict of murder by person or persons unknown, Coroner J Tolver Waters said, 'The deceased was apparently a respectable girl although she might have gone out with young men' and 'might unwisely have chosen young men above her station'. He called the case 'a dark mystery'. Local gossip maintained the answer lay with the yachting fraternity, but rumour begets rumour, only fading with time. Did Chief Constable Parker consider calling in Scotland Yard, as he had done with Mary Bennett? Possibly he saw the case as purely local and may have delayed long enough to make a request impractical.

In October the police thought the case was solved. George Ward, a 23-year-old fisherman, strongly built, six feet tall with haggard features, walked into Litcham Police Station and announced he had murdered Dolly Gray; and he knew Dolly – had been out with her on at least three occasions and was said to be 'greatly enamoured of her'. And he had been missing from Yarmouth after the murder. On 10 October he appeared before Yarmouth Magistrates charged with her murder. On 23 October the charge was withdrawn and he was committed to the workhouse as insane. Dolly's body had been found early on 15 July, dead only a few hours. Ward had been arrested in Holbeach, Lincolnshire, at 10.30 pm on 14 July for begging and sentenced to fourteen days imprisonment, the time and distance factors seemingly irreconcilable – his absence from Yarmouth now explained.

In proposing the innocence of Herbert Bennett, supporters have connected the murders of Mary Bennett and Dolly Gray. Would Bennett have been convicted if a similar unsolved case had existed? If he had been acquitted would that have been as much an injustice as the failure to find Dolly Gray's killer?

CHAPTER 9

The New Century

The Heigham Murder, 1905

Sudden and violent death may be horrifically revealing yet leave the possibilities of accident, suicide and murder in abeyance. A knife between the shoulder blades or a bullet hole in the back of the head *prima facie* cries murder; other scenes may be less indicative. Some cases immediately point to murder and the murderer, there being no other candidates, and such was the case known to Norwich citizens as the Heigham murder. It featured the raw emotion of domestic strife, a gruesome death and a seemingly obvious murderer, but it had an unforeseen conclusion, if conclusion it really was.

In 1905 the Norwich district of North Heigham was mainly residential and working class, a sameness of orderly rows of streets and terraced houses in which Railway Street formed a short cul-de-sac running from Heigham Street to a meadow and the railway line from the nearby City Station. The Kowen family lived at 29 Railway Street, the last house before the meadow. A century later all has gone, swept away by industrial development.

James Kowen, aged thirty-eight years, worked as foreman drover at the cattle pens at the City Station, also running a general dealer business with Albert Cooper of Barn Road. James, known to everyone as Jimmy, was a respected member of the Liberal Association, the Catholic League and the Foresters, but that respect did not extend to his marital life. Neighbours heard quarrels in 29 Railway Street and his wife had been seen with bruises and a black eye, which she openly attributed to her husband.

Rosa Kowen was born Rosa Davy in Norfolk in 1866 and married James Kowen in 1891. She was described as a 'dressmaker of imperfect education', a big woman, dark-haired and sallow-faced, coarse and foul-mouthed when roused. She often complained to neighbours that her husband did not allow her enough money, speaking of him in scathing terms and threatening to leave him and go to London. Prone to gossip, she had made the meaningful statements: 'I'd have a good drink if he was brought in stiff' and 'I shall have done something to him'. Albert Cooper heard her tell her husband, during a furious quarrel, 'I will be hung for you'. Rosa told a neighbour she hated the sight of her husband and he should be in an asylum. On the occasion when she sported a black eye she claimed that she had done her bit by breaking a chair and a door in the skirmish. That she was a powerfully built woman would be the subject of some important discussion.

There were two Kowen children: Reginald, aged twelve years, and

Clifford, aged four years. How much they suffered through the domestic strife around them would be argued by opposing lawyers accusing father or mother as it suited. Maria Hastings (misnamed Haystead in several reports), a domestic help aged fifty years, said she saw Rosa strike Reginald across the face with a cane when she was 'in drink'. Unquestionably Rosa was 'in drink' on 22 December 1905 when she came home and found she had been locked out. She called and hurled stones at a window, rousing neighbours but leaving her husband unmoved. He was heard to declare, 'I will not have the drunken old cow in my house.' Eventually, with the street in thrall, Reginald came down and let his mother in.

Rosa pawned clothes, blankets and her rings, unashamedly using others to carry out the errands. She said she wanted to augment her housekeeping. Some thought she wanted money for alcohol. She was assisted in and around the house by Maria Hastings and George 'Yankee' Edwards, Hastings carrying out domestic chores and Edwards more physical duties such as chopping wood and looking after livestock. Edwards slept in a shed on the meadow. Hastings visited twice a week and was paid by Rosa, incurring the wrath of Jimmy, who thought his wife could do more about the house (employing a domestic help in this working-class environment was unusual).

During the afternoon of Thursday, 28 December 1905, William Hindle, a solicitor's clerk and friend of Jimmy Kowen, called at 29 Railway Street to invite Jimmy and Rosa to accompany him to the theatre that evening. As Jimmy hesitated, Hindle said that Reginald was old enough to be left to look after Clifford.

Jimmy Kowen replied, 'I would not leave my children for a hundred pounds. Supposing a fire were to happen. I should never forgive myself.' Rosa said nothing. Maria Hastings would say that Rosa was 'in drink' that afternoon but Hindle thought she was sober.

The evening of 28 December was cold, damp and moonless. Jimmy Kowen went to his office at the cattle pens and Yankee Edwards saw him there at eight-thirty. He was next seen at the *Orchard Tavern* in Heigham Street, where he ordered two pennyworth of whisky, an unusual order for Jimmy. Landlord William Wilkins would describe him as 'abstemious', regularly ordering 'ginger beer and a packet of fags'. Jimmy paid for his whisky from a Melford (wrap-over) purse, seen by Wilkins to contain two half-sovereigns and eight or nine silver shillings, an observation that would later exercise legal minds.

At a quarter to eleven Jimmy met Albert Cooper in Barn Road. They parted at a quarter past eleven and Jimmy was not seen alive again, except by his wife. She spent part of the evening gossiping with her neighbour, Mary Tills, at their respective back gates, going indoors at a quarter past nine.

Mary Tills lived with her husband, Arthur, and daughter Ethel at 27 Railway Street, and Ethel's bedroom abutted the bedroom of Jimmy and

Heigham Street in the early twentieth century, unrecognisable today. Railway Street was on the left, beyond the horse and cart. Norfolk County Council Library & Information Services

Rosa Kowen. On this particular evening Ethel came home late and dallied outside her house with her boyfriend, Mark Greenfield. They parted at midnight, observing that the Kowens' bedroom light was still on. At ten minutes after midnight Ethel, preparing for bed, heard knocking on her partitioning wall. Rosa Kowen's voice cried, 'Ethel! Ethel! I believe my house is on fire.' Ethel roused her mother and father.

Samuel Grand, a railway loader of 26 Railway Street, heard cries from across the street and, opening his bedroom window, saw Rosa at her open window crying that her house was on fire. Seeing Grand she cried, 'Jimmy, where is he? Is he on the meadow or is he with Cooper?' Grand's head-on view did not reveal a fire but the children were now at the window crying 'Fire! Fire!' Throwing on some clothes Grand ran across the street, joined by James Jeary from 25 Railway Street. Arthur and Mary Tills went in search of a policeman.

Standing under the bedroom window, Grand urged Rosa to drop the children into his arms and this was successfully accomplished. Rosa next threw her cash box into the hands of Mrs Jane Grand. Samuel Grand then placed a plank against the window and Rosa, fully dressed but with her blouse irregularly fastened, scrambled down.

Running to the back of the house, Samuel Grand had the alarming experience of stumbling over the Kowens' dog, renowned for its noisy alertness and ferociousness, matters to be of some note. Untangling himself from an unhappy canine, he burst through an unlocked back door into a living room, which he described as 'dimmed with smoke.' He recoiled from the heat of two fires. A natural fire burned in the grate, more than reinforced by rogue flames leaping from a bonfire of clothes, cushions and a tablecloth on the floor several feet away. Pressing a wet cloth over his face, he slouched forward, suddenly joined by Constable Thomas Gardiner. James Jeary backed up and fed in pails of water.

Samuel Grand and Constable Gardiner peered through the smoke, seeing the vague outline of a burning man lying on his back, the right arm on the grate fender and the left side against the flaming clothes. Crouching and fending off smoke and heat, they dragged the clothed but flaming body through the suffocating atmosphere into the back yard, both suffering begrimed faces and singed eyebrows and hair.

Outside in the clearing air the body lay in full exposed horror, burnt down one side, the arm flexed in the common fire death position, the face blackened and disfigured. A bloodied, smashed skull completed the revolting picture.

Rosa had been taken into 27 Railway Street, where she told Mary Tills, 'I believe my house is on fire. I don't know whether my husband is indoors or not. I heard him go out; but I did not hear him come in', a statement that does not sit easily with her next explanation to comforting neighbours, which she repeated to the police. She said that her husband had come home, joined her in the bedroom, removed only his collar and then said because there was a nice fire in the hearth he would go downstairs and read for a while. She said that because of her neuralgia she buried her head in the pillow but after about twenty minutes she heard a 'lumping sound and breaking glass' and went down to find the room on fire.

Chief Constable Edwin Winch and Chief Engineer Stanley Shaw arrived from the Pottergate Fire Station with the horse-drawn fire appliance to find the flames had been doused by pails of water. The Norwich City Police had triple roles of police, fire and ambulancemen, and the chief constable, required to attend all fire call-outs, arrived as a fireman and metamorphosed into a policeman. This was no ordinary fire.

The arrival of the police surgeon, Dr Robert Mills, and the Head of CID, Detective Inspector Charles High, showed police thinking. Soon Detective Sergeant Henry Goldsmith would be added to the investigating officers. The blood-soaked and burnt body, by now dragged into the front room of the house, proclaimed murder.

The living room of 29 Railway Street was not for the faint-hearted. Blackened and scorched walls and blistered doors enclosed the lingering smell of smoke and burnt flesh. A partially burnt settee and pile of charred clothes bordered a dark patch on the floor, marking where the seat of the fire had burned through a rug and lino into wooden planking. Moving the remnants of the rug gave off a smell of paraffin. Clothes stacked against the body included the overcoat Jimmy Kowen had worn that evening, normally placed on a hook behind the door to the staircase. Much of the burnt material was now unrecognisable leading to later argument as to what exactly had been there.

A pool of baked blood lay near the seat of the fire. More blood could be seen on the hearth fender and by the door leading to the staircase, and there were blood splashes on the walls. Jimmy Kowen's boots stood in isolation, splashed with blood. The living-room table, minus table-cloth, had been moved from the centre of the room to a position by the pantry door and it was bloodstained at the front and underneath. A half-sovereign and hammer lay on the mantelpiece, the latter looking singularly out of place though inquiries would show that it was used to break up coal and was in its usual position. But it had been washed! Removing the hammer-head revealed traces of blood.

In the scullery police found an empty paraffin can. Inquiries would trace Sarah Webster of Railway Street, aged twelve years, who on Boxing Day had purchased two pints of paraffin for Rosa Kowen.

Detective Inspector High discovered a bloodstained chopper and axe in the coalhouse with blood smeared on the coalhouse wall. In 1905 crime investigation was still in the 'if it looks like blood it is blood' era, even though rudimentary blood grouping had been discovered. Unfortunately, the detailed analysis that would benefit crime detection was still many years away. But it looked straightforward at 29 Railway Street. There was undisputedly blood all over the place and a bloodied body. That four-year-old Clifford Kowen had been treated for a nose bleed that evening seemed a small matter in the light of his father's bloodstained corpse.

Neighbours comforting Rosa in 27 Railway Street told her of the body and expressed the opinion that it was Yankee Edwards. She refused to look at the body, saying it must be her husband because Yankee would not be there at that time of night. She could have had another reason for believing the body belonged to her husband.

Chief Constable Winch thought the fire had been burning twenty to thirty minutes before discovery. He waited for Dr Mills to confirm other matters he was already sure about. The police surgeon did not disap-point. His post-mortem examination at the city mortuary in King Street revealed numerous blows to one side of the head with a sharp instru-ment, and more on the other side and to the forehead involving a blunt instrument. There had been a heavy blow to the back of the head. He found several depressed fractures and a hole in the front of the head with part of the brain protruding. There was evidence of twenty-six blows in all. He opined that after receiving the injuries Jimmy Kowen could have lived no more than fifteen minutes. He thought all three bloodstained weapons could be related to the injuries. The hammer fitted exactly into some of the wounds.

Removing the clothes from the body produced nine shillings and sevenpence ha'penny from a trouser pocket but no Melford purse or half-sovereigns as seen by the landlord of the *Orchard Tavern*. The insides of both

James Kowen, victim, sketched from a photograph. David Rowlands

trouser pockets were bloodstained, as if a bloodied hand had been thrust inside.

Chief Constable Winch interviewed Rosa at 27 Railway Street on the morning of the death and would say that she demonstrated an air of complete indifference to the loss of her husband. She repeated her story of Jimmy coming home and going downstairs to read by the hearth fire, received with scepticism by the chief constable. He and Detective Inspector High believed she was the murderer and she must have noted their suspicion. Later that day she asked Maria Hastings if 'the tecs' had been to see her.

Rosa did not remain a free woman for long. The police had what they thought to be a strong case, enhanced when they examined her clothes. Her blouse showed red spots that had been sponged. On the Saturday afternoon Chief Constable Winch arrested and cautioned her. She replied, 'I didn't murder him. I am not guilty.'

Charged before the magistrates, she tempered her initial reply, saying, 'I did not plan to murder him nor hurt him in any way.' If you examine her words carefully they make sense if you consider a sequence of argument, fury and a total loss of normal reasoning. Would she plead provocation or insanity? It seemed she couldn't dispute the facts. Who else could have killed Jimmy Kowen? A reputed ferocious and noisy guard dog had remained undisturbed until Samuel Grand fell over it. It must have been an in-house murder.

Jimmy Kowen's funeral took place on 3 January 1906, leaving his sister's house in Spencer Street supposedly in secret but soon followed by a growing crowd of several hundred. He was buried at Earlham cemetery next to the Catholic chapel, and Canon Duckett in his eulogy spoke of him as 'well-known and widely respected'.

Beginning on 18 January, the police called witnesses and presented evidence to magistrates. After hearings totalling twelve hours and twenty minutes Rosa Kowen was committed for trial at the Winter Assizes.

After several inquest adjournments, starting at *The Waterman* public house (inquests in public houses were now frowned upon by the Home Office, which didn't stop them continuing for another half-century), a full hearing of seven hours took place at the Guildhall. Witnesses, fresh from the committal, repeated their evidence and a jury adjudicated under the guidance of Coroner Mr R Ladell. (Later years would see a coroner's jury resolving cause and manner of death only after another jury had resolved guilt or innocence).

After a short retirement the jury foreman announced, 'We are agreed that the deceased James Kowen died from injuries inflicted by his wife Rosa Kowen.'

Coroner Ladell exclaimed, 'That is murder!'

Foreman: 'Yes.'

The coroner duly returned a verdict that Rosa Kowen murdered her husband. Would the Assizes jury agree? The evidence seemed conclusive.

A Norwich Special (arranged for one case) Assizes commenced on 14 March, the venue moved from the Guildhall to the Shirehall to provide greater accommodation. A large crowd queued at the doors heedless of falling snow, some waiting to gain entry, some waiting to see the prisoner arrive in a horse-drawn cab from Norwich Prison. A significant number of women could be seen in the outside crowd and later in the public gallery.

Rosa Kowen appeared in the dock dressed in black, gazed round the crowded courtroom and burst into tears. Mr Justice J C Lawrance gave her permission to sit down. Mr Horace Avory (later Sir Horace and an eminent judge) led for the prosecution and Mr Ernest Wild (later Sir Ernest and Recorder of London) for the defence.

Rosa pleaded 'Not Guilty'. Her defence was simple: she didn't do it. Mr Wild began to dismantle prosecution witnesses and sow seeds of doubt. He started with the evidence of Rosa's drinking. James Jeary said all the overheard quarrels stemmed from her drinking and Maria Hastings said that Rosa spent long hours in 27 Railway Street with Mary Tills, drinking pints of beer and hastily returning home when the boy Clifford warned of the approach of her husband. Mary Tills said this was untrue and the Tills family as a whole cast Rosa in a more sober light, which allowed Mr Wild to undermine the evidence of Jeary and Hastings. He saw the evidence of Hastings as the more damaging and riled her in cross-examination, provoking her into sharp replies to show she was motivated by a dislike of Rosa Kowen. He disputed that Rosa struck Reginald with a cane and queried Maria's account of Rosa throwing a chair at her husband, producing a chair from 29 Railway Street and asking whether the prisoner could possibly have thrown such a heavy piece of furniture. Maria Hastings had no doubt: yes, she could!

Mr Wild sought to improve the image of his client and devalue the presumption of an in-house murder. He used the missing Melford purse, believed to have been destroyed in the fire, as a pointer to a burglar and asked Samuel Grand what happened after he fell over the 'ferocious' guard dog. Grand said the animal ran away, which amused the public gallery but achieved Mr Wild's aim. Yankee Edwards went one better. He told the court that the dog was useful only for herding livestock and would let anyone pass. So much for a reputation garnered through

Rosa Kowen, accused.

neighbours fed-up with the animal's barking.

Chief Constable Winch told the court that there was no sign of smoke on the wallpaper on the staircase next to the living room, indicating that the door had not been opened while the fire was in progress, as claimed by the prisoner. He produced a bloodstained brick taken from the coalhouse wall, which, he said, showed that somebody bloodstained had touched the wall as they replaced the chopper. Mr Wild disdainfully asked if his evidence was theoretical. The chief constable agreed it was.

Mr Wild elicited from Yankee Edwards that he had recently used the chopper to chop wood, but failed to get him to admit the possibility that he may have nicked his hand in doing so. As far as Yankee was concerned it was not his blood on the chopper, a disappointment for Mr Wild.

Dr Mills spoke in detail of twenty-six wounds, incised on one side of the head and dented on the other. He described frontal injuries in which the nasal bone had been broken and driven-in and all the upper teeth knocked out. He had found, he said, a contusion on the chest caused by 'considerable violence' and another on the neck, possibly related to a throttling attempt. He spoke of bloodied pockets and was sure the red spots on the prisoner's blouse were blood, and equally sure they had been sponged. During his evidence Rosa began sobbing and several women hurriedly left the courtroom.

The jury were taken to 29 Railway Street to view the geography of the house, and a photographer, Edgar Wilkinson from the Royal Arcade, produced photographs of the scene. Another step into the future came from the use of a Home Office pathologist, although his evidence didn't help the prosecution. Augustus Pepper didn't think the axe had inflicted any of the wounds but had acquired bloodstains from touching the main weapon, the chopper. He thought the chopper and hammer related to the wounds, and the blows had been struck with great force, consistent with delivery by a man. In his opinion a woman assailant needed a large swinging circle, something not conducive to such a small room. He agreed that he had not been called to the case until 19 February but said he had examined parts of the victim's skull. It seems that Jimmy Kowen was not buried intact.

Pepper said the bloodspots on the prisoner's blouse were, to be

Chief Constable Edwin Winch, investigator. Norfolk
Constabulary Archives

precise, blood*stains*, and they had been sponged.
And he had visited the scene and found a trace of
blood on the bottom step of the staircase. He produced a wood shaving showing the blood. The
inference was that the murderer had gone that way.

Mr Avory summed up for the prosecution,
firmly telling the jury that it was beyond dispute
that the deceased had been brutally murdered and
the first blow had clearly been struck from behind,
and the fire was intended to destroy evidence of
the crime. He averred the prisoner's guilt, there
being no other possibility.

Mr Wild said there was no dispute over the facts
but a 'book of remembrance had been opened
against the prisoner' with 'inferences, conjectures
and suspicions'. He said Maria Hastings had been
given to 'feminine exaggeration'. He spoke of a ferocious dog that had proved to be a 'pacific dog',
adding, to gallery amusement, 'so out goes the dog'.
He asked whether anybody 'in that slaughterhouse'
could have escaped being heavily bloodstained, which the prisoner had not
been. He said that all the prosecution had on Rosa Kowen was a few spots
on her blouse, probably caused by her four-year-old son sneezing from a
bleeding nose. He referred to the missing Melford purse, asking, 'Where
was it?' and scornfully adding, 'Whenever the prosecution got into difficulty they burnt things on the fire.' He finished by saying the murderer
appeared 'more man than woman'. His speech, described by the *Norfolk
Chronicle* as a 'fine peroration', was a powerful attempt to erode overwhelming evidence of guilt. The judge's summing-up restored the weight
of prosecution evidence.

Mr Justice Lawrance was dismissive of the defence's intruder theory.
He pointed out that a murderer lighting a fire would quickly draw attention to his crime. He asked why he would do that when he could be miles
away before the body was discovered. And why would a stranger replace
the hammer on the mantelpiece? And go to the trouble of taking the
chopper and axe back to their original positions? He reviewed the overall evidence but his scepticism over a possible intruder seemed to doom
Mr Wild's eloquence.

The jury had been accommodated during the trial in the *Castle Hotel*.
Now, at two o'clock on the afternoon of the third day, they retired to
consider their verdict. They took longer than expected, not returning
until twenty-five minutes past four.

Ernest Wild, an eloquent defender.

The Clerk of Assize formally intoned the question 'Have you reached a verdict upon which you are all agreed?'

The jury foreman said they hadn't reached a unanimous verdict and the judge then asked, 'Is there any chance of you agreeing?'

The foreman replied, 'I think not, my lord.'

Mr Justice Lawrance discharged the jury, ordering their freedom from jury service for seven years, and committed Rosa Kowen back to Norwich Prison to await the next Assizes. We can only wonder how the twelve men good and true were divided. Was there just one stickler? Where did the balance lie – to convict or acquit? Two hours and twenty-five minutes is not long for a jury retirement by today's standards. Would the majority verdict of the future, a minimum of ten agreed after two hours, have helped? We shall never know.

At the Norwich Assizes on 16 June, Rosa Kowen faced a new jury and judge. Mr Justice A T Lawrence presided. Mr Horace Avory again prosecuted and Mr Ernest Wild again defended, except that he no longer led for the defence. Mr F K North appeared as defence leading counsel and began by challenging five of the jurors. They were replaced.

Again the defence strongly advocated an outside murderer, now in greater detail. They saw a man entering 29 Railway Street from the back, having accessed the road from the meadow. Mr North questioned witnesses to elicit that Jimmy Kowen and Albert Cooper ran a business likely to attract 'rough customers', and the business was doing well and Jimmy often carried a considerable sum of money, not just for the business but for the Foresters. His Melford purse had apparently contained £20 on 20 December. William Hindle gave evidence that, a few days before Christmas, geese kept in the back yard had been killed and there had been much blood spilt. It is not clear whether the defence were claiming a goose-killing intruder or attempting to cloud the issue of blood found in the coalhouse. Dr Mills thought the blood on the chopper and axe was 'mammalian'. The jury again visited 29 Railway Street.

Before Maria Hastings was called, Mr North objected to her giving evidence that she saw Rosa strike Reginald Kowen across the face with a cane when 'in drink'. He said it was prejudicial, in other words it was not relevant to the charge and told against his client. The judge agreed and ordered the prosecution not to adduce the matter.

Mr North, prompted by Mr Wild, made Rosa's disposition to drink seem inconsequential and, with the aid of Mary Tills, again refuted the evidence of Maria Hastings that drinking sessions took place in 27 Railway Street. Maria again suffered in the witness box, more so this time. She sobbed as Mr North questioned her to show that she had her own domestic crisis. She had little money and had been forced to pawn several of her possessions, and her husband had recently been committed to an asylum. Since the last trial she had spoken to the chief constable about clothes worn by Rosa Kowen that were missing, the inference being they had been bloodied and gone on the fire. Mr North made the most of this witness collaboration between trials, showing that Maria Hastings had a desire to convict Rosa Kowen.

During her cross-examination on the subject of Rosa's clothes Maria Hastings lapsed into a tearful, head-bowed silence and refused to speak. Mr North badgered her and asked why she didn't answer his repeated questions. She eventually replied, 'I'm worried.'

Mr North fired back, 'So is that poor woman in the dock.'

Having shown Rosa in a better light than some witnesses had proposed, Mr North made much of a lack of motive, saying that Rosa's total financial gain from the death of her husband was £53 10s, plus some furniture insurance, hardly enough to commit murder for. This was a political diversion because nobody had said she murdered for money. The facts suggested it was an impulsive act spurred by rage.

The inability to prove that the blood on the hammer, chopper and axe came from the victim was of no account because the defence said that an outsider committed the murder; nevertheless, Mr North did say that the blood on the chopper could be years old, which again shows the limitations of forensic science of the time.

At the end of the second day the jury asked if they might be allowed some fresh air before being returned to their hotel. The judge agreed. At another point in the trial the foreman asked that they be supplied with smelling salts. Again the judge agreed.

Mr North handed over to Mr Wild for the defence closing speech and this persuasive and articulate gentleman spoke for two and a quarter hours, emphasising the fearful injuries and blood-spattered scene and, as before, pointing out that Rosa had only a few spots on her blouse, devaluing prosecution witnesses and claiming there was no apparent motive, again denigrating a useless guard dog, again suggesting that everything pointed to a burglarious entry. Wild's biographer would refer to this closing speech as 'a hurricane of eloquence'. At the very end Wild implored the jury: 'Can you imagine this poor woman sitting here could be transformed suddenly into a fiend in human shape and one of the most brutal murderers that history has ever told of?'

Mr Justice Lawrence summed up and, like his predecessor, scorned the suggestion of a burglar, saying there was 'nothing to indicate the presence of such a criminal', and it did not make sense to hang around and light a fire and draw early attention to the crime. He said of Rosa, 'Was her conduct that of an innocent person?' He questioned why she took no action to extinguish the fire knowing, as she must, that her husband was in danger. He wanted to know why she had taken time to light candles before calling for help and why she had called out asking where her husband was when she knew he was downstairs. He told the jury not to worry about circumstantial evidence because you could 'not expect a host of witnesses' to such cases; and as for there being no adequate motive, crimes were often committed with an inadequate motive. He was not persuaded by Mr Wild's point that Rosa's clothes did not relate to the blood-spattered scene, expressing the view that if she had committed the murder she could have burned her clothes on the fire, the charred contents of which had never been fully identified. Rosa Kowen must have been resigned to see him wearing the black cap later in the day.

Mr North asked if the jury could take the chopper with them when they retired.

The judge replied in the stilted language peculiar to his profession, 'Not without they ask for it'.

The jury promptly asked for it, and the clothes and chair exhibits as well. The judge agreed.

The jury retired at ten minutes to four on the afternoon of the fourth day. They returned at twenty minutes past six, almost the same time lapse as the first jury. To the chagrin and astonishment of many, including the judge, the foreman announced they could not agree.

Mr Justice Lawrence asked if there was any chance of them agreeing.

The foreman replied, 'None whatever, I regret to say.'

The judge discharged the jury, exempted them from jury service for seven years, and ordered a composed Rosa Kowen back to Norwich Prison.

Before the court rose Mr Justice Lawrence announced that defence lawyers had praised Chief Constable Winch for the 'fearless and fair manner' in which he had dealt with the case and he, the judge, wished to endorse that praise.

On 5 July 1906 the Attorney General sent identical telegrams to the prison governor, chief constable and Mr W E Keefe, solicitor representing Rosa Kowen. An order of *nolle prosequi* (we shall no longer prosecute) instructed Rosa's release. The prosecution had had enough. The evidence appeared substantial, unlikely to improve, and two juries had failed to convict upon it.

Rosa received the news in the morning that she was a free woman. Newspapers had already carried the news, and a few people, the press and the curious, idled outside the prison awaiting her release, speculating whether she would go to her children, staying with friends, or to Railway Street.

It seems that Rosa received advice from the prison governor and Mr Keefe that her presence in Norwich would be fraught with difficulty. Such advice accords with a view of Rosa as a symbolic battered wife, perhaps a rallying figure for the stirrings of women's suffrage, on the other hand a hated person perceived to have got away with murder, a divisive figure leading to trouble in the streets. It is, of course, possible that Rosa had already decided what she wanted.

Just before three o'clock in the afternoon a cab containing Mr Keefe and Rosa's father arrived at the prison. It was a quick turnaround. The cab left the prison at 'a rattling pace' followed by reporters, travelling straight to Norwich Thorpe Station. At half past three on the afternoon of 6 July 1906 Rosa Kowen, described by the *Eastern Evening News* as 'the most talked-about woman Norwich has known for a generation', left the city on a train to London's Liverpool Street Station, her destination from there a secret (she had a sister in London). Many would say she escaped a city and justice. Not entirely, as we shall see.

The *Eastern Evening News* had staked out 29 Railway Street, where their reporter found no curiously waiting neighbours or sensation-seeking onlookers, just a lone policeman and a child playing in an otherwise empty street. The house stood locked and desolate. In the back yard a forlorn dog lay, shorn of a reputation, head between paws, staring at a water bowl, flicking its eyes at the peering reporter, who in the absence of anything else to report would record finding 'a dog subject of much forensic eloquence', presumed by the reporter to be fed and watered by the police: more likely Yankee Edwards. Before the end of the month the furniture and effects of 29 Railway Street would be auctioned, attracting as many souvenir-hunters as dealers or bargain-hunters. The fate of an amiable dog is not recorded.

The Norwich Watch Committee recorded their appreciation of the work of the police officers in the case and elevated Detective Inspector High, Detective Sergeant Goldsmith and Police Constable Gardiner to higher grades of pay. They praised Chief Constable Winch, noting 'the admirable manner in which he prepared and presented the evidence at two Assizes' trials', awarding him £5 'out-of-pocket expenses' and another £5 to be distributed among the other officers at his discretion. High died suddenly in 1910 while still a serving officer. Winch later suffered from scandal and retired on ill-health grounds in 1917. Goldsmith retired in 1911. Gardiner retired in 1928 with the rank of Inspector.

There is an ending that might be seen as justice for Jimmy Kowen and illumination for two juries. Rosa Kowen's freedom lasted only two weeks. Following an 'incident' that 'caused fear to those near to her' she was committed to the London County Council Asylum and certified as insane. A fitting end perhaps; a guilty verdict at Assizes might have given the same result. She was later transferred to the Hellesdon Hospital at Norwich and remained there until her death on 4 February 1927. She lies in Earlham cemetery at a considerable distance from her husband.

CHAPTER 10

Epilogue

Murdered on Duty, 1907 & 1909

Duty is epitomised by the police service, recognised by statutes that forbid obstruction and assault. In Norfolk a number of officers have died executing that duty. Some fell through accident or misfortune, struck down by the tragedy of unforeseen circumstances, but three were murdered.

Constable William Callow of the Norwich city force was felled in a riot in Norwich in 1848, to die from his injuries, his assailant never discovered. His tale is told in *Norwich Murders*. The deaths of Constable Walter Ford of the county force, based at Edgefield, and Constable Charles Alger of the Great Yarmouth borough force, based at Gorleston, came in the early twentieth century, only two years apart, arising from incidents they saw as routine, if anything can ever be routine in police work. Walter Ford was not even a regular officer but a parish constable, a non-uniformed appointment that had been the forerunner of the professional police and only gradually declined in rural areas, and he was not even on duty, although there is a view that police officers, in whatever form, are always on duty.

Edgefield lies a few miles from the towns of Holt and Melton Constable, comprising secluded and scattered dwellings in tranquil surroundings, seemingly a place where not much happens. In the early hours of Sunday, 30 June 1907, tragedies of the severest kind marred this peaceable hamlet.

Constable Walter Ford had spent the previous evening shopping and socialising in Holt with his wife Georgeama and they returned to their cottage at The Green in Edgefield quite late. They prepared and ate a meal and it was near two o'clock in the morning when Walter went outside to fetch some coal. In the darkness and silence of a country night he came upon events that were to take his life.

Walter Ford was thirty-seven years of age, a blacksmith as well as a custodian of the peace. In respect of the latter he had been considering what to do about William Jacobs, who lived in Ramsgate Street in the village with his 74-year-old father and had of late been a nuisance. Jacobs junior, a labourer, had been known for his 'lively, jocular disposition' but lately he had 'taken to religion' and pestered villagers with his beliefs, and on Friday his employer had sent him home from Melton Constable

Constable Walter Ford and Mrs Ford.
Cromer & North Walsham Post

because of his frantic behaviour. Contrary to his employer's instructions he returned to work the next day and such was his demented and intense manner nobody would go near him. Ford knew he would soon have to try and calm Jacobs. He little knew as he went to fetch coal that the time had come.

Ford halted midway to the coalhouse as a voice from the next-door garden pierced the silence. Rhoda Batchelor and her 21-year-old son George lived next door and the voice did not belong to either of them. Ford moved to the separating fence as Rhoda and George Batchelor opened a window in response to the voice. The time was ten minutes past two. William Jacobs junior stood in the Batchelors' garden, shouting and gesticulating.

Jacobs yelled, 'Salvation! I want you, George, because you are the right man. I can see a shining light and I am going to heaven.' Seeing Walter Ford at the fence, Jacobs called, 'Well, Walter, how are you getting on?' and 'Will you come? I will show you the light.'

Ford spoke reassuringly to 'Billy', as he called him, and Billy invited him to come over the fence to be converted. Seeing Mrs Ford in the doorway, he offered to convert her as well. She shrank away and urged her husband not to go over the fence but he said he was a constable and had a duty to soothe the man. He climbed over the fence and began chatting to Billy. Mrs Ford, with a sense of foreboding, went to seek help.

Walter Ford was tall and well built, and Jacobs was much shorter and of slight build, a disparity that meant nothing as Jacobs, with the element of surprise, seized and threw Ford to the ground, falling upon him and furiously striking him in the back. The rising and falling hand held a small knife. The watching George Batchelor (who was Ford's nephew) quickly put on a shirt and trousers and rushed to the constable's aid.

Batchelor grappled with the knife-wielding man and received a flurry of blows to the head. He reeled away with a gaping wound across his

forehead. Jacobs followed him, slashing and stabbing as he chased him back to his cottage. Walter Ford crawled towards his own garden but Jacobs returned, stabbing him again and again in the back, only breaking away as voices and figures loomed out of the darkness. Jacobs ran through a hedge and disappeared.

Mrs Ford and Charles Lock, a young stockman, helped Walter Ford into his cottage, where he collapsed, gasping to his wife, 'Oh my dear, I am dying, I cannot move. I am bleeding so. William Jacobs has done it.'

Lock left to summon the police and a doctor but surgeon Robert de Beavois did not arrive until five o'clock. He dressed Ford's wounds, which included a large cut to the scalp, small cuts to the hands and numerous puncture wounds in the back. Walter Ford died at twenty minutes to seven that morning.

Constable Moore arrived from Baconsthorpe and Constable Wright and Inspector Robert Flint from Holt. A trampled potato patch in the Batchelors' garden yielded a bloodstained pocket knife and a cap belonging to Jacobs. Constables Moore and Wright went to look for Jacobs and found him standing by a field gate near the main road (this is the evidence of Constable Moore – press reports claim Jacobs was hiding in a garden shed). He offered no resistance as he was arrested, informing the constables he had seen 'the devils of the night' and, more ominously, he had intended to 'kill fifteen or sixteen people who did not have the faith' and, 'I have been cutting and slashing the whole night. I must have killed two men.' He had.

Charles Lock had moved on to rouse John Hagon, brother-in-law of William Jacobs, and together they went to inform Jacobs senior of his son's attack upon the constable. They found the Jacobses' cottage silent, dark and secure. Receiving no response to his knocking and calls, Hagon unlocked the door and entered, to recoil from a scene of utter carnage.

William Jacobs senior lay in the passageway to the kitchen soaked in blood, his head cleaved open and his brains splashed across the kitchen floor and wall. A blood-covered meat cleaver lay on the floor. Trousers and a waistcoat had been discarded nearby, covered in blood and brains.

William Jacobs junior. Cromer & North Walsham Post

Inspector Flint, called to the cottage, found more blood on the staircase and in the bedroom. The picture was of the old man felled by repeated blows from the cleaver and the blood-spattered assailant changing his clothes before leaving. So Walter Ford had approached what he presumed to be a trespassing religious fanatic, in reality a demented murderer.

The constables held Jacobs junior in a carpenter's shop until Inspector Flint arrived, Jacobs greeting the inspector with, 'I have killed my old chap. The lord helped me do it.' Villagers gathered outside the shop and as Jacobs was led through them to a carriage he gesticulated and laughed. He was taken to the Beckham workhouse and placed under guard for the night.

The facts were horrible, tragic, but straightforward. So straightforward that surgeon de Beavois did not think post-mortems were necessary. Coroner Mr W Barton disagreed and ordered post-mortems. The examination of Ford revealed that he had received a four-and-a-half-inch wound to the head that had taken off his scalp, and thirty-eight stab wounds to the back, four of which had penetrated a lung. None of the wounds were singularly fatal and he had died from the cumulative affect of shock and haemorrhage.

William Jacobs senior's injuries had been inflicted with massive force. The left half of the head, face and jaw had been hacked away and the right side of the head and face had been fractured, and 'the brains were missing'. Everyone was appalled by the ferocity of the injuries, inflicted by a slightly built man, a son who had previously enjoyed an amicable relationship with his father.

Magistrates sat at Holt on the Wednesday and heard evidence from witnesses, Mrs Ford fainting three times. Jacobs remained calm, occasionally making obscure comments.

When his sister, Esther Hagon, gave evidence he asked, 'Are you frightened?'

She replied, 'No, Billy.'

Jacobs said, 'Then why are you shaking? You will do me in if you don't mind.'

Constable Charles Alger. Norfolk Constabulary Archives

George Batchelor gave evidence shakily, his head heavily bandaged.

The magistrates committed Jacobs to the next Assizes for trial and he was taken by train to Norwich Prison, alternating between moods of calm and sudden violence, sometimes frothing at the mouth. His victims were buried in the parish churchyard at the end of the week.

The inquest opened on Monday, 1 July, in the village schoolhouse, under Coroner Barton, and adjourned to 27 July, but before then, on 16 July, Jacobs was committed to Broadmoor Lunatic Asylum on an order from Norwich Prison certifying him as 'a dangerous lunatic'. The inquest jury, under the foremanship of the vicar, the Reverend Walter Marcon, duly recorded that Walter Ford and William Jacobs senior 'died from injuries inflicted by W Jacobs who was of unsound mind'. The Assizes at Norwich granted an application to adjourn all witnesses *sine die.*

The village of Edgefield recognised the bravery of Walter Ford and George Batchelor by instituting the Ford Relief Fund, from which Mrs Ford would receive regular payments as long as the fund lasted. The Reverend Marcon presented Batchelor with £4 for his 'unselfish bravery'. Walter Ford had done his duty when he was not on duty and in doing so had probably saved the lives of others.

★★★

No question that Constable Charles Alger was on duty when as a uniformed beat policeman in the Great Yarmouth borough force he sought to resolve a domestic dispute, a duty familiar to every police officer. Alger was thirty-seven years of age and in 1909 he had a wife and four children and fourteen years' creditable police service. He was known in Gorleston-on-Sea as the friendly copper on the beat.

A visitor may see Gorleston as an extension of Great Yarmouth, but to its residents it was, and is, a proudly separate, bustling community with its own pier, beach and holiday facilities. On a showery afternoon, on 18 August 1909, Gorleston and Constable Alger made policing history, the most tragic kind.

Restoring the peace in a fractious household may be seen as routine in policing terms, and often the parties concerned are already known to the peace-restoring, umpiring officer. Alger knew Thomas Allen, a vermin-catcher, as a petty thief, poacher, drunkard and, significantly, a man who had previously assaulted him. Allen was fifty-six years of age, of scrawny and diminutive build, narrow-eyed, balding and wispy-bearded. His eleven children had all left home and after living at various addresses from which he had been evicted or persuaded to leave for 'quarrelling and misconduct' he had for two or more years lived with his wife, Barbara, at 12 St Andrew's Road, Gorleston, next to the recreation ground.

On the historic afternoon, Mrs Agnes Cox of 8 St Andrew's Road heard a scream and a female voice calling, 'Murder! Help!' She saw Thomas Allen outside his house, hitting his wife with what looked like a rusty piece of a gun.

Mrs Cox ran forward and pulled Mrs Allen away, the crying woman fleeing into Mrs Gray's house at 1 St Andrew's Road, and that lady, suitably alerted, quickly bolting her doors. Allen tried to follow but was delayed by Mrs Cox attempting to wrest the gun from his grasp.

Allen shouted, 'That's all right. That's all right!' and squirmed free and banged on Mrs Gray's door. Mrs Cox pulled him back shouting, 'For God's sake, don't! I implore you. Give it to me.'

Allen ran into his own house, reappearing in his back garden grappling with something in his hands. He had what Mrs Cox described as 'a mischievous look' on his face. She set off for the police station.

At a quarter past four Mrs Cox reported the incident at Gorleston Police Station in the High Street. Inspector Walter Moore, in charge of the station, dealt with the report in the manner of the time. He sent a constable to deal with the matter. Charles Alger was available because he was about to start his beat at the riverside. Exactly what Mrs Cox said at the station is not recorded but neither Inspector Moore nor Constable Alger saw the matter as especially dangerous. A renowned poacher belabouring his wife with a rusty piece of gun would not inspire the police response of today, which is not a criticism of old or new times.

Mrs Cox walked with Constable Alger to St Andrew's Road and, content that the officer would soon deal with Thomas Allen, she went into her own house. As is the case when a uniformed policeman appears in suburbia, other residents took an interest.

Alger found Thomas Allen prowling his own back garden, 'marching up and down' according to one witness, and without a gun, rusty or otherwise. He wore a slouch hat and appeared unfazed by Alger's arrival. In the traditional all-time opener of an arriving policeman Alger asked Allen what was 'going on', walking forward as he posed the question. Rain began to fall.

Allen replied, 'Come into the garden and I'll tell you,' a redundant invitation because Alger was already coming. The two men met in the back garden, spoke and walked a few paces. Mrs Agnes Popay of 26 St Andrew's Road watched an encounter she designated 'friendly' until, suddenly, in a swift movement, Allen reached down to a potato patch and straightened up holding one-handed what looked like a pistol. In fact it was a double-barrelled shotgun, shortened to about twelve inches, the stock cut back to the trigger, a weapon useful for pocket storage by a poacher. Allen held the gun at arm's length, pointing it at Alger. Mrs Clara Woodhams of 24 St Andrew's Road thought the gun to be almost at touching distance to the constable's throat.

Mrs Popay heard Allen say, 'If you do not clear out I will shoot you.'

Alger had no chance to 'clear out', or reply. Allen fired, the shot punching a large hole in Alger's neck, the report echoing along the road and across the recreation ground, turning heads and bringing people to windows and doors, and onto to the road and recreation ground. Mrs Cox ran into the road, filled with apprehension.

Alger turned with the blast and looked towards Mrs Popay, gasping as if trying to say something. Blood poured from his throat. He staggered towards the road, stooping, his helmet spilling to the ground.

Allen snapped open the gun and reloaded, saying, 'I have finished one and I have another one over here.' He stepped over the low wood-and-wire fence into the recreation ground, walking towards the pavilion, ignoring the uniformed figure struggling to stay upright.

William Bullock, a painter working at 31 St Andrew's Road, heard the gunshot and traced it to Allen's garden where he saw the constable 'stooping, trying to walk'. Bullock ran forward to help the stricken man, joined by Charles Hammond, a tram driver about to go on duty. Bullock led Alger to the fence and tried to hold him up as he slowly collapsed. Hammond tried to unfasten the constable's tunic collar, part of which had been blown away, but the constable's neck had swollen and the collar could not be freed.

George Warner, the recreation ground attendant (he lived at 30 St Andrew's Road), alerted by the shot, saw Allen walking towards the pavilion, carrying what he thought to be the barrel of an old pistol. Then a boy ran past shouting that a policeman had been shot. Warner opened a gate leading to St Andrew's Road and saw two men (Bullock and Hammond) bending over a prone figure. He ran to help, closely followed by Mrs Popay and Miss Muriel Lankester, a visitor who had been sheltering in the pavilion from the rain.

Events that followed were, owing to their suddenness, shock and general confusion, recalled slightly differently by all the parties concerned, but together they made a coherent statement of events.

Mrs Cox saw Allen backtracking from the recreation ground, looking intently at the fallen constable and the people clustered round him. She shouted, 'For God's sake, look out! Here he comes again!'

Hammond looked up and saw Allen looking directly at him, 'holding a pistol by his side'. Hammond could not be sure whether Allen said, 'I want another one' or 'It's another one I want', the difference being academic. Inspired by perceived danger Hammond tried to jump over the fence into the recreation ground but tripped and fell over it. He heard a shot and Mrs Cox shouting, 'Don't go back; he's loading again!'

Bullock heard Mrs Cox's first warning and saw Allen approaching. He thought Allen said 'You are there, are you?' Bullock scrambled over the fence and heard the shot.

Warner, bending over the fallen constable, saw Allen about ten yards away without appreciating the danger. He concentrated on what he described as 'trying to break his [Alger's] collar adrift' until he felt a blow to the head and thought he had been struck with a stick. He put his hand to the right side of his head and found the flesh ragged and bleeding.

Warner stood up, looked at Allen, and said, 'What are you up to, Tom?'

Allen replied, 'Oh, you are one of them.'

Warner climbed over the fence and, dazed, staggering, his face covered in blood, was hustled away by helpers. Miss Lankester ran away with wounds to her hand. Mrs Popay limped away with wounds to her leg and she and Warner were taken by horse-drawn cart to the Gorleston Cottage Hospital.

Alger rolled over with the new shot, convulsively raising and lowering his arms, but he was beyond recovery. The first shot had done for him.

Induced by horror and sensation, and aided by juvenile fitness, two boys made speedy progress to Gorleston Police Station to breathlessly report terrible happenings. Inspector Moore collected Constable Arthur Tink and Constable George Orford, a close friend of Alger, and set out at a brisk pace for St Andrew's Road, the officers arriving at a fast trot to carve their way through a growing but wary crowd. The days of blue lights and sirens, armed officers, loud hailers, taped cordons and trained negotiators belonged to a far-off age.

Tink went to the back of 12 St Andrew's Road without seeing Allen, while Orford covered the front. Inspector Moore went along the side of the house and saw Allen stepping away from him, going behind the house. Moore followed. Allen stopped, facing Moore, holding the gun in front of him. Moore could see Alger lying near the fence, grievously injured if not dead. He advanced slowly and steadily upon Allen.

Walter Moore was fifty-two years of age, married with seven children and nearing the end of his service. A long and successful career would shortly be rewarded with a pension and more equable lifestyle, if he lived. This was not a stand-off based on bluff, a man posturing with a dummy or unloaded gun. People had been shot and the man who had shot them was pointing the gun at Inspector Moore. Would one more make any difference to the gunman? Moore kept advancing.

Moore called, 'Allen, you had better give in. I am going to have you. You had better surrender.' Perhaps this first verbal contact would not be in the present-day negotiator's manual but Moore knew his man. He followed up in a firm voice with, 'Put the revolver down'. (He didn't know he was facing a shortened shotgun).

Allen called back, 'Come on old Moore. I shan't hurt you.' Moore kept on.

Moore had spoken firmly, asserting authority in a tense confrontation, closing the distance between him and the gun as he talked. At a distance where a touch of the trigger would have brought certain death, Moore reached forward and gripped the weapon with his left hand, grabbing Allen's free left arm with his right hand. Allen released the gun. It was over.

A cry went up, 'The inspector has got him!' and civilians and police rushed forward. Moore handcuffed his prisoner.

Arthur Tink and George Orford lifted their fallen colleague into a horse-drawn cart and set out at a gallop for the Cottage Hospital. Matron Gertrude Marsters, forewarned, received them at five o'clock and detected a flicker of life in the badly injured constable, but as she began to organise medical help she realised the flicker had gone. Constable Alger was dead.

Dr John Reed, surgeon to the hospital, attended at half past five and certified death. The following day he conducted a post-mortem with Dr Percy Gilmour and described a wound in the right side of the neck, one and a half inches long and an inch wide, very deep, reaching down to the main arteries and blood vessels. He found three cartridge wads and numerous shot in the wound. The carotid artery was riddled with shot and the jugular vein had been practically destroyed. The skin was lacerated around the wound and contained more shot. Nearly thirty shot were extracted, others were left. Death had resulted from shock and haemorrhage. Medical opinion was that Alger might have lived half an hour, more probably a quarter of an hour, and no medical aid at any time could possibly have saved his life.

The doctors found evidence of only one gunshot. Two were definitely fired, some witnesses, and consequently historians, would have three or more. William Smith, a gardener at the recreation ground, gave a newspaper interview claiming that after shooting the constable Allen went towards the pavilion intent upon shooting him [Smith] because of an earlier dispute, and did fire at him and miss. Whilst this would explain Allen heading towards the pavilion, and some of his remarks, Smith's account was not supported by witnesses and did not go beyond a newspaper interview.

Two shots were certainly fired at Alger, one fatally at close range, the other after he had fallen and been approached by helpers. A shortened shotgun can cause terrible injury at short range; less so with distance.

They found their colleague shot and dying: Constable Arthur Tink, left, and Constable George Orford, right. Norfolk Constabulary Archives

The second discharge caught Warner, the two women and Alger, and came over several yards. Doctors estimated the range of the fatal shot to Alger's neck as a few inches.

Warner's injuries were such that his condition was initially described as 'precarious'. He had between twenty and thirty shot in the right side of his head, face, neck and shoulder, one going through his cheek into his mouth. He slowly recovered and left hospital on 30 August.

Agnes Popay's injuries were described as 'serious', mainly shot wounds to her legs. She gradually recovered at home, carrying pellets in her leg for the rest of her life. Miss Lankester was treated for minor wounds.

When Allen was searched two live cartridges were found in one pocket, an empty cartridge in another pocket. Another empty cartridge was found in the potato patch, all supporting the fact of two shots only. The gun was loaded with two live cartridges. One of the triggers was broken and one barrel, although loaded, was incapable of firing.

Allen was conveyed to Great Yarmouth Police Station by four officers and interviewed by Chief Constable Parker.

Allen asked, 'Is he dead?'

Chief Constable: 'Yes.'

Allen: 'It's all through her.' He was charged with the murder of Constable Alger, and later the attempted murder of George Warner.

The inquest took place at Church Road Boys' School under Coroner Mr J Tolver Waters, and the jury were taken to view the body and the garden. In giving his evidence Inspector Moore produced Alger's torn and bloodied tunic. Mrs Cox became so distressed in the witness box she had to be assisted from the hearing. A juryman thought Allen's wife should be present to say whether her husband was 'in drink', as Mrs Cox

Constable Alger's funeral. Leading figures include Inspector Moore, left, and Chief Constable Parker, centre with stick. Norfolk Constabulary Archives

thought and Inspector Moore doubted. The coroner said that was a matter for the Assizes and asked the juryman to withdraw his request. He did and the jury returned a verdict of 'Wilful Murder' by Thomas Allen.

Mrs Allen gave a newspaper interview in which she said that, before Mrs Cox intervened, her husband fired at her and the pellets struck her backside. She also said that Alger spoke to her before confronting her husband and she warned, 'Mind he has a gun', and he replied, 'Oh! Has he', a statement rather than question.

Constable Charles William Alger was buried on 23 August, the procession leaving his home at Trafalgar Road West for St Andrew's Church and Gorleston cemetery. Thousands lined the route, and hundreds took part in the procession, which was led and followed by mounted officers. Business establishments shuttered their windows; houses drew curtains. The mayor and other dignitaries, and representatives of many local institutions, attended the service to pay their respects. The Reverend Forbes-Phillips told the congregation, 'Poor Alger was an example of that kindly nice way and manner that is characteristic of the police force in England.' A packed churchyard remained unmoved by heavy rain. At the graveside his wife stood forlornly with two boys, the eldest aged eight years, and two little uncomprehending girls. That afternoon and evening a steady, unremitting stream of people walked past Constable Alger's grave.

The *Yarmouth Mercury* began a public subscription for the widow and children, starting with their donation of one guinea, and the mayor instituted a relief fund. A letter to the press demanded that the corporation provide for the family, saying it was their 'bounden duty'. The Yarmouth Hippodrome circus put on a special benefit performance for the family.

Thomas Allen made three appearances before magistrates, the last on 2 September – the first occasion George Warner was fit enough to give evidence. On each occasion the courtroom was packed to capacity with a large outside crowd hooting and jeering Allen's coming and going.

Agnes Cox twice fainted as she gave her evidence. She identified the shotgun used to shoot the policeman but caused surprise when she said it wasn't the one Allen was hitting his wife with. There was no evidence that another gun existed and the presumption seems to have been that she was in error in not twice identifying the weapon.

Allen, looking pale and dishevelled according to the press – a state not far removed from his normal appearance, was undefended. He declined to ask questions but made a strange remark, perhaps a clue to his likely defence.

He said, 'I wish to have this case decided by the planets and we will see who is right or wrong.' (He had recently consulted an astrologer.) The magistrates formally committed him for trial and he was taken to Norwich Prison by train. The question in most minds was not of innocence or guilt but whether he could escape the gallows. It seemed unlikely. The evidence pointed to a cold-blooded killing without provocation.

At the Norfolk Assizes on 29 October Allen pleaded 'Not Guilty', although it was never in dispute that he had killed Constable Alger. Mr A Lombe Taylor appeared for the defence and Mr Montague Beaumont Monce for the prosecution. Mr Justice Lawrance presided.

The prosecution evidence deviated little from the committal and inquest evidence. Mr Lombe Taylor questioned witnesses to show that Allen had behaved irrationally (who would doubt that?) and put forward a defence of insanity, seeking to save his client from the hangman. To this end he called his star witness: Dr Craig, a 'physician in mental diseases' at Guy's Hospital, London. This worthy gentleman had interviewed Allen in Norwich Prison on two occasions but before giving his evidence he warned that what he had to say would be unpleasant to ladies. The judge said he couldn't see any ladies. Nevertheless, the Clerk of Assize took it upon himself to order any ladies present from the court.

It is difficult to see what in Dr Craig's evidence would have upset Edwardian ladies. The chivalrous doctor spoke of Allen suffering from delusions that his wife was conducting affairs with various men and in consequence he was going to 'sting' these men with his shotgun. Apparently the astrologer seen by Allen had claimed she would get twelve months if she revealed all she knew about his wife. (Some records have interpreted the astrologer as saying Mrs Allen would get twelve months.) There followed a three-cornered cut-and-thrust

A press montage showing Allen in the dock, centre, standing – not seated as captioned (a picture that would today be in contempt of court), and, top right: George Warner; bottom right: Inspector Moore; top left: Constable Alger (his name misspelt); bottom left: Agnes Popay. Norfolk Constabulary Archives

between Dr Craig, Mr Beaumont Monce and the judge as to why Allen should have shot a policeman who had nothing to do with his wife, the difference between stinging and killing, and whether the actions under discussion proved insanity.

Dr Craig said that Allen had explained to him he was 'only going to frighten him [Alger] but the unguarded trigger went off accidentally'. The doctor said that Allen did not believe he would kill anybody by shooting them. (This from a poacher!)

Pushed by the judge as to whether he thought Allen was truly insane, Dr Craig said, 'I consider he had probably been of unsound mind for several years.'

The question of what constitutes insanity in a particular case can have psychiatric experts arguing from different sides and lawyers and judges variously interpreting legal guidelines. In this case the prosecution did not have a psychiatric expert to argue with Dr Craig.

Mr Lombe Taylor, in his closing speech, underlined Dr Craig's evidence and asked, 'Would a man of sound mind attempt to act as the prisoner has acted?'

Mr Beaumont Monce told the jury, 'Neither on the ground of drunkenness, nor of delusions, nor of insanity, can you find that the prisoner, who is a violent man, is innocent of the crime with which he is charged.'

The judge summed up by pointing out that the facts were not in doubt and the whole case hinged on whether the prisoner was responsible for his actions, whether he knew and understood what he was doing when he shot Constable Alger. He said that insanity could be total or partial.

Delusions from a temporary aberration of the mind would eventually find a place in the Homicide Act of 1957, offering a defence of diminished responsibility and a consequent manslaughter verdict, but in 1909 the jury simply had to decide whether Thomas Allen was not just bad, they knew that, but mad as well. They took half an hour to decide that Allen was sane and guilty of murder.

Mr Justice Lawrance addressed Allen, saying, 'The jury rightly came to the conclusion that you are guilty of the crime of murder, a murder committed under circumstances of the greatest cruelty ….'

Allen interrupted: 'I didn't intend to do that man any injury at all, sir.'

Mr Justice Lawrance did not fall into the trap of arguing with a convicted man. Wearing the black cap, he told Allen,

> Assuming for a moment – although I don't believe it and have no evidence or grounds to believe it – that your belief with regard to your wife was correct, nothing could justify you shooting that unfortunate policeman who came to protect your wife from your violence.

He sentenced Allen to be hanged, a sentence that left Allen unmoved.

The date was fixed. Thomas Allen would hang at Norwich Prison on 16 November, or would he? Defence lawyers took the views of Dr Craig to the Home Secretary, Herbert Gladstone (son of the famous Lord Gladstone), and a Home Office letter ordered that Thomas Allen

Inspector Moore with his medal.
Norfolk Constabulary Archives

IN

LOVING MEMORY OF

CHARLES WILLIAM ALGER,

WHO DIED AUG. 18TH 1909,

AGED 37 YEARS.

"LEAVE THY FATHERLESS CHILDREN
I WILL PRESERVE THEM ALIVE
AND LET THY WIDOW TRUST IN ME"

Constable Alger's headstone shows an angel bending over a fallen policeman. Les Cole

should be subjected to further medical reports, and in consequence he would be reprieved and committed to Broadmoor Lunatic Asylum. A detached Home Office view had overridden a judge and jury that had listened to the evidence first-hand.

Allen had undoubtedly been fixated by thoughts of his wife's infidelity, of which there was not the slightest evidence, but what had that to do with him shooting a policeman? The answer probably lies with his dislike of authority and, in particular, of Alger, whom he had previously assaulted. Today lawyers could consider a diminished responsibility defence. Certainly he could not be hanged.

For his bravery Inspector Walter Moore received the King's Commendation for Conspicuous Gallantry, the police officer's Victoria Cross, and who would say he had not earned it? He had looked at death and survived. He retired in 1912.

Constable George Orford died in 1914, aged forty-three years, and was buried alongside his friend and colleague, Charles Alger.

Thomas Allen never gained his freedom. He died on 15 February 1920 in Rampton Mental Institution, aged sixty-seven years.

Charles Alger of Gorleston and Walter Ford of Edgefield remain historic icons, murdered on duty, doing what police officers are regularly required to do. They never saw the end coming; it was just another duty. George Henderson published a poem after Alger's death. A verse is reproduced here as a 21st-century tribute.

Let us pity the poor fellow
Who has lost his life on duty bound
He has died the life of heroes
Which, thank God! are sometimes found

Bibliography

Abbott, Geoffrey. *William Calcraft*, St Albans, Verulam Publishing, 2004.

Blackham, Robert. *Sir Ernest Wild K C*, London, Rich & Cowan, 1935.

Braithwaite, J B, ed. *Memoirs of Joseph John Gurney*, 2 vols, Norwich, Fletcher & Alexander, 1854.

Butcher, Brian. *A Movable Rambling Police*, Norfolk Constabulary, 1989.

Capon, Paul. *The Great Yarmouth Mystery*, London, Harrap, 1965.

Evans, Stella. 'The Life and Death of Richard Nockolds' in *Swing Unmasked: the Agricultural Riots of 1830 to 1832*, Ed. Michael Holland.

Gurney, J J. *Account of John Stratford*.

Mackie, Charles. *Norfolk Annals*, Norfolk Chronicle, 1901, vol. 2, 1854–1900.

Monbiot, R. *The Burnhams Book of Characters and Memories*.

National Archives – depositions, letters

Norfolk Heritage Centre, Millennium Library – records and reports

Norfolk Record Office – letters, statements, prosecution papers

Norwich Castle Study Centre – depositions, letters, prosecution papers

Phillips, Bernard. *The Burnham Murderers*, 1981.

Riches, J. *The Burnham Murderers*, 1836.

Tooke, Colin. *Great Yarmouth – The Rows and the Old Town*. Great Yarmouth, Tooke's Books, 2000.

William White's 1845 Gazetteer and Directory of Norfolk, David & Charles Reprints.

Cromer & North Walsham Post

Eastern Daily Press

Eastern Evening News

Norfolk Daily Standard

Norwich Argus

Norfolk Chronicle and Norwich Gazette

Norwich Mercury

Yarmouth Independent

Yarmouth Mercury

Illustrated Mail

The Times

Minutes of Great Yarmouth Council and Watch Committee, King's Lynn Watch Committee, Norwich Watch Committee

Index